Teaching English Overseas:
An Introduction

Also published in
Oxford Handbooks for Language Teachers

Teaching English Overseas: An Introduction

Sandra Lee McKay

OXFORD
UNIVERSITY PRESS

Oxford University Press, Great Clarendon Street, Oxford OX2 6DP

Oxford   New York
Auckland   Bangkok   Buenos Aires   Cape Town   Chennai
Dar es Salaam   Delhi   Hong Kong   Istanbul   Karachi   Kolkata
Kuala Lumpur   Madrid   Melbourne   Mexico City   Mumbai
Nairobi   São Paulo   Shanghai   Taipei   Tokyo   Toronto

Oxford and *Oxford English* are trade marks of
Oxford University Press

ISBN 0 19 432814 7

© Sandra Lee McKay 1992

First published 1992
Fifth impression 2003

Set in Adobe Garamond

Printed in China

CONTENTS

ACKNOWLEDGEMENTS

Many people contributed to the completion of this book. Thomas Kral, Thomas Miller, and Dee Parker, all English Teaching Officers for the United States Information Agency, shared with me their resources and experiences in supervising English teaching in various countries. Georgene Lovecky of the Council for International Exhange of Scholars made available to me the final reports of several Fulbright lecturers. Diane Larsen-Freeman provided me with master's theses on teaching overseas done at the School for International Training. Many expatriate teachers, like Jay Charlesworth, Michele Dubarry, David Kluge, and Anthony Tassinari, shared with me their personal accounts of overseas teaching. Indigo Crone and William Kumai, two of my graduate students, provided me with valuable feedback on the manuscript. Henry Widdowson offered constructive and tactful suggestions on the various drafts. I am most grateful to all of these individuals for their assistance on the project. Finally, I wish to thank my family for their support while I was teaching overseas gathering material for the book, and while I was writing it.

The author and publishers would like to thank the following for permission to reproduce copyright material: Addison Wesley Publishing for an extract from *Skill Sharpeners* (1984) by J. DeFilippo and C. Skidmore; Prentice Hall for a table from *Principles of Language Learning and Teaching* (2nd edn.) (1987) by H. Douglas Brown; TESOL for an article by Susan Lewis English from *TESOL Newsletter* 23/1.

Every effort has been made to trace the owners of copyright material in this book, but we should be pleased to hear from any copyright holder whom we have been unable to contact.

INTRODUCTION

The proliferation of terms for describing the teaching of English to non-native speakers includes TESL (the teaching of English as a second language); TEFL (the teaching of English as a foreign language); TEIL (the teaching of English as an international language), and TEAL (the teaching of English as an auxiliary language). This attests to the wide variety of contexts in which English is currently being taught. Yet few methodology texts address the manner in which the larger context affects language teaching. The purpose of this book is to explore the way in which the teaching of English in non-anglophone countries is influenced by social, economic, cultural, educational, and institutional contexts. It is addressed to in-service and pre-service teachers who intend to teach English in countries where it is not spoken natively.

This book makes several assumptions about teaching overseas. First, it assumes that English teaching is an activity infused with social and political significance. Decisions regarding who learns English in a country, in what context, and for what purposes, are all made within the political arena. Deciding who learns English can have important social consequences such as maintaining the status of an élite, or aiding in the eradication of a minority language. Because of the social and political significance of teaching English, expatriate language teachers need to become aware of the manner in which English operates in the country in which they are working or about to take up a post. For example, who determines who learns English? Who supports the teaching of English, and for what purposes?

Second, the book assumes that schools both reflect and reinforce cultural values, whether these values involve an emphasis on individualism, competition, collectivism, or collaboration. The roles of teachers and learners, the content of curricula, and the choice of methodology all reflect the cultural values of a country. The book also assumes that expatriate teachers need to become aware of their own cultural biases regarding what constitutes good teaching, and to recognize that other perspectives may be equally valid.

Finally, the book assumes that the role of expatriate teachers, as guests of a host country, is not to effect change in its social and educational structure, but rather to attempt to increase their students' proficiency in

English as best they can within the existing structure. If expatriate teachers are philosophically opposed to existing language policies in a country, they have two choices: either they can decide not to teach in that country, or they can elect to teach in an institution which challenges existing policies by providing classes to those not typically allowed or encouraged to learn English. If expatriate teachers are philosophically opposed to the curriculum and methodology of a school, they have two choices: either they can seek employment in another teaching context which is more compatible with their own views, or they can negotiate with the school administrator and students to arrive at an alternative methodo-logy that is acceptable to all.

There are several things which this book is not designed to do. First, since it is not feasible to discuss all of the countries where English is currently taught, it does not provide teachers with detailed accounts of all possible English teaching situations. Rather it discusses representative case studies as a way of introducing important issues related to the teaching of English overseas. Also, the book does not deal with the practical aspects of settling in a new country, such as finding a place to live or using local transportation. While these are important factors in teaching abroad, the focus of this book is on the professional rather than the practical concerns of employment overseas. Finally, it does not deal with the general area of cultural adjustment, again an important concern, but one that is a whole focus of investigation beyond the scope of this book; however, sources for readings on this topic are suggested.

The countries dealt with in the 'Case studies' section of each chapter are included because they provide clear illustrations of the theoretical topics covered in the first part of the chapter and/or because extensive research has been done in these countries regarding the use of English. The case studies which relate the teaching experience of individual teachers are intended to illustrate the diversity of teaching situations that exist overseas and the various responses that individuals can have to the professional context in which they find themselves. They represent particular examples of overseas teaching experience, reflecting one individual's perspective. Thus, they should not be used to form simple generalizations about teaching abroad, generalizations that could easily result in misconceptions or stereotypes. While generalizations are needed to deal with overseas teaching, they need to be grounded in research and reflection.

I recognize that no account of overseas teaching can be totally objective. In discussing the cultural and educational values of other countries, I am inevitably revealing my own; other authors cited in the book do the same. While I argue throughout the book that language teachers need to strive to put aside their own cultural biases, to see each culture in its own right, and to respect its characteristics, the fact that cultural differences exist below the surface, often out of one's awareness, makes the goal of total objectivity difficult, if not unattainable.

This book is divided into two main parts. The first explores how the larger context—the social, political, economic, and cultural arena—affects the teaching of English, while the second investigates how a country's educational and institutional structure affects it.

Part One, 'The larger context', examines questions such as the following: How are decisions regarding the role of English made in a country? How do sentiments of national identity and a desire for political stability affect such decisions? How do economic incentives affect individual motivation for learning English? How do such incentives influence the spread of English and the domains in which it is used within a country? How do cultural values affect the roles of teachers and students? What cultural topics should be included in the curriculum?

Part Two, 'The educational context', deals with educational issues which include the following: What is the role of a country's Ministry of Education in formulating language education policies? What standard of English should be taught in schools in non-anglophone countries? What are the advantages and disadvantages of a standardized national curriculum? What types of institutions provide English teaching in non-anglophone countries, and how do they differ? What questions should language teachers ask employers before accepting a teaching post?

All of the chapters include questions for discussion, as well as topics for research projects. In addition, they provide a list of suggested reading for those who wish to explore particular issues further. Included at the end of the book is a glossary of key terms which should be particularly useful to individuals who are new to the field of language teaching.

PART ONE

The larger context

1 LANGUAGE TEACHING AND THE SOCIOPOLITICAL CONTEXT

Theoretical background

In many countries throughout the world, teaching English is an activity infused with social and political significance. As Judd (1987:15) notes, simply by teaching English as a second or foreign language, we are 'directly or indirectly implementing a stated or implied language policy as well as actively promoting a form of language change in our students.' In some countries, policies regarding the teaching of English may be based in part on a desire to restrict knowledge of the language to an élite, while in others the study of English may be promoted as a basis for achieving political unity or economic development. In either case the choice of who is or is not allowed to learn English is often made within the political arena, with teachers playing a key role in carrying out the policy.

In this chapter we will explore how the social and political context of a country affects English language teaching. The chapter will begin by describing the process and benefits of language planning. Next, the formation of language policies will be examined in light of both a country's desire to promote a national identity (*nationalism*), and the practical concerns of governing (*nationism*). Finally, the language planning of three specific countries will be discussed in terms of nationalism versus nationism. Throughout the chapter, emphasis will be placed on how the role of a language teacher is affected by decisions which relate to language planning.

Language planning

Definition of language planning

According to Rubin (1983:4), language planning is deliberate language change which is based on the identification of a language problem. There are two dimensions to language planning: *status planning*, which changes the function of various languages within a society, and *corpus planning*, which is undertaken to develop a language so that it can have more functions in a society. Corpus planning can include such things as expanding the vocabulary of a language, determining a standard of usage, or developing a writing system. These two types of planning often occur together since decisions which alter the status of a language can also necessitate some type of corpus planning.

One of the major decisions that a country may face in terms of status planning is the designation of an official language or languages. Once a language has been chosen for this purpose, it is typically used by a government for its internal operations, for such functions as recording laws, conducting parliamentary proceedings, or operating the courts (Conrad and Fishman 1977:8). As we shall see in Chapter 2, one of the reasons for the spread of English is that it has been designated an official language in a large number of former United States and British colonies. Because English has been afforded official status in these countries, knowledge of the language has become an essential qualification for obtaining many government positions and therefore individuals are anxious to study English for economic betterment.

If a nation decides to designate an indigenous language as an official language rather than one of wider communication like English, corpus planning may be needed to standardize and modernize the language. For example, in 1930, when several East African countries agreed to work together to standardize and modernize Swahili so that it could be used as the language of education, the Zanzibar dialect of Swahili was chosen as the standard which was to be promoted throughout the region. An East African Swahili Committee was established to standardize the orthography of the language, control the publication of dictionaries and standard grammars, secure uniformity in usage and syntax, and translate selected books into Swahili (Eastman 1983:227). As we shall see in the 'Case studies' section of this chapter, similar corpus planning has been undertaken in Malaysia with Bahasa Malaysia so that the language can be used in place of English in government and education.

In the case of English, corpus planning is an important issue in terms of what variety of the language to promote. In countries like the Philippines, India, and South Africa, where English has some official status and is used widely, new varieties have developed. The question facing language planners in these countries is what variety of English to promote as the standard—the local variety, or a variety that is used in a country where English is the primary language, for example, the United States, the United Kingdom, or Canada? The issue of varieties of English is one which will be discussed in depth in Chapter 4.

Language-in-education planning

Language-in-education planning occurs when political leaders determine such things as what language to use as a medium of instruction in the schools or to require as a subject of study, what objectives to specify in the language curriculum, or what standard of usage to promote in educational materials. In terms of status planning, the question of what language to use as the medium of instruction in schools is one of the major decisions in language-in-education planning. While an important conference sponsored by Unesco in 1951 recommended that every effort should be made to provide initial education in the mother tongue, in many countries today this recommendation is not followed, either because political leaders wish to promote the use of a language of wider communication such as English, or because the mother tongue is not sufficiently developed to be used as a medium of instruction.

In order for a language to be used effectively as a medium of instruction, the following conditions are necessary: first, the language must have an accepted writing system; second, basic teaching and reading materials must be available in the language, and finally, there must be teachers who can speak, read, and write it well enough to teach it (Bowers 1968:388). If a language does not meet these criteria, then either corpus planning must be undertaken to modernize it for use in schools, as is currently being undertaken in Malaysia, or a language of wider communication such as English needs to be chosen as the medium of instruction. In Chapter 4 we will examine the issues surrounding the designation of a medium of instruction in schools.

The process of language planning

Paulston (1983:55-6) distinguishes three stages in the language planning process that can be applied to both status and corpus planning: determination, development, and implementation. In this model, *determination* involves initial decisions regarding what language policies to implement, both in terms of the functions of given languages within a country and of the development of the language itself; *development* entails the elaboration of the means to achieve the desired outcome, and *implementation* is the actual attempt to bring about the desired goals. Particularly important for teachers is the distinction that Paulston makes in language planning between language *cultivation,* which is concerned with matters of the language itself and involves decisions by language specialists regarding corpus planning, and language *policy,* which is concerned with matters of society and nation and involves decisions by government officials and agencies regarding both status and corpus planning. Paulston contends that although decisions regarding language cultivation are made by language specialists, they are frequently judged in light of language policies determined by government officials. Let us examine how Paulston's model might be applied to language-in-education planning.

Imagine that in a particular country the Ministry of Education, the policy-making body, decided to undertake an English textbook reform project (step one). The Ministry might begin by asking a group of language specialists to write a new series of textbooks. The textbook commission would, in turn, begin by determining guide-lines and policies for the preparation of the series (step two) before actually writing it (step three). After the textbook commission developed the series, the books would then need to be submitted to the Ministry of Education for final approval (step four). If the series were approved, the Ministry would then decide how to best implement its use in the schools (step five). Figure 1.1 illustrates these five steps in the textbook reform project, demonstrating the interplay between politicians and language specialists.

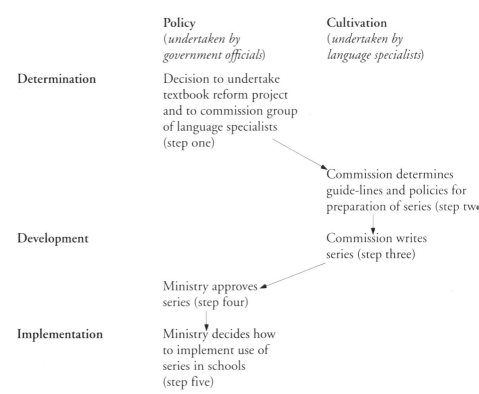

Figure 1.1: Five steps in a textbook reform project (adapted from Paulston 1983:60)

Paulston (ibid.:62) maintains that while an evaluation of work produced by language specialists in regard to language planning should be made by other language specialists, often such decisions are made instead by government officials. The political realities of a particular country may dictate a result very different from that deemed most appropriate by the language specialist. For example, in the hypothetical case of the textbook series, while the series could be excellent on linguistic grounds as judged by the language specialists, if in content the books ran counter to the political or religious ideology of the country, they might be rejected by the political leaders. (In fact, Paulston (ibid.:63) cites the example of a textbook commission in Peru whose work was rejected by the Ministry of Education, necessitating the formation of a whole new commission.) Thus, in many instances, the work of language specialists may be ultimately judged by reference to political rather than linguistic or pedagogic criteria.

In making judgements about the appropriateness of a language plan, Paulston (ibid.:65) contends that 'government officials do not often base language decisions on language data either out of ignorance or because political considerations are given precedence.' Thus, the opinions of language specialists may be ignored if their views are not in keeping with the political goals of a nation. Paulston provides the following example of how a language specialist's opinion was superseded by a policy decision:

> A Canadian language specialist was asked to evaluate the foreign-language teaching system in an Arab nation in the Middle East. As the medium of instruction at the university level is English and the students have difficulties with it, he suggested that they consider English instead of Classical Arabic as the medium of instruction during the last two years in high school. The suggestion was promptly rejected for reasons of nationalism and religion, symbolized by Classical Arabic. The government official understood very well the merit of the suggestion for increased efficiency of English teaching, but for him efficiency of English teaching was not the primary function of high-school education. It is crucial in evaluating educational language planning that one consider the function of education in that society. The linguist readily accepted the decision; it was not within his domain to question the function of education of that nation. Some time thereafter, however, another government official became Minister of Education, and he saw the practical merit of the language specialist's recommendations. Consequently, a programme, carefully evaluated, is now being carried out, which uses English as the medium of instruction, and which promises to become a model programme for similar situations. (Paulston 1983:64)

What is most instructive for expatriate language teachers from this example is the fact that the Canadian linguist readily accepted the decision of the government hierarchy, recognizing that it was not his function to question the rationale for educational policies in the society even if he believed the policy was not in the best educational interest of the students. The linguist recognized that language cultivation, in Paulston's terms, will always be subject to policy approval in which political issues may well take precedence over pedagogic ones. As Hartshone points out in reference to South Africa:

> language policies are highly charged political issues and seldom if ever decided on educational grounds alone. . . . This is particularly true of the experience of bilingual and multilingual countries, among them South Africa, where decisions on language in education have to do with issues of political dominance, the protection of the power structure, the preservation of privilege and the distribution of economic resources. (Hartshone 1987:63)

Since educational issues are bound to be affected by political decisions, expatriate language teachers need constantly to be aware of how the conditions of the wider context are affecting language-in-education planning.

Benefits of language planning

Why does a country undertake language planning? According to Jernudd and Das Gupta (1971:206-8), language planning can result in several benefits to a society. First, by providing a certain degree of linguistic homogeneity, it can allow for quicker and better communication, and a consequent increase in the standard of living. Second, language planning, in so far as it produces a common means of communication, can result in greater equality of participation in the society.

These two outcomes are considered benefits only if a society wishes to allow equal access to economic and political power to all of its citizens. In some cases, a government may promote a language-in-education policy which restricts economic and political power to a few. For example, during the 1950s and 1960s, South Africa had a Bantu Education policy in which mother-tongue instruction was used in all black South African schools. Since this policy limited students' literacy in both English and Afrikaans, the two official languages, many black South Africans viewed it as a way of restricting their access to economic and political participation. In teaching a particular language that has economic and political power in a society, language teachers become part of the political process. If this language happens to be English, and if opportunities to learn English are largely restricted to the élite, then teachers of the language are helping to maintain the status quo. Because of this fact, expatriate language teachers need to be aware of their role in the political structure of a country in order to determine whether or not they wish to become part of that country's political process.

According to Jernudd and Das Gupta (ibid.:206-8), a final benefit of language planning is that, by promoting the use of a particular language, it can foster a sense of national consciousness, thus strengthening the political unity of the country. Ironically, as we shall see in the case of Malaysia, sometimes the promotion of a national language undermines rather than strengthens political unity, demonstrating the complex relationship between language planning, nationalism, and political unity. It is this issue that we turn to now.

Nationalism versus nationism

Language planning is closely related to Fishman's distinction (1968:43) between nationality-nationalism and nation-nationism. Within this framework, 'nationalities' are groups of people who view themselves as a sociocultural unit with integrative bonds, whereas 'nations' are political units which tend to have one dominant nationality. In determining language policies, Fishman contends that a country needs to balance the concerns of *nationalism* (the feelings that develop from a sense of group identity) and *nationism* (the practical concerns of governing). If language policies are formed primarily on the basis of nationalism, in which the concern of promoting a national identity is paramount, such things as the efficient conduct of the government and its institutions may suffer. On the other hand, if language policies are based on nationism, with little regard for the emotional attachment that languages can have, language planning may engender great hostility among some members of society. Hence, while it may be more efficient to have one language spoken throughout a country, such a decision may be met by great resistance by those who speak and cherish another language.

A-modal nations

In discussing the language planning of post-colonial multilingual developing nations, Fishman (1969) distinguishes three types of nation. In the first type, *A-modal nations*, countries which have an oral rather than a written tradition, language choices are made with the goal of achieving political unity through language planning. Often such countries select a language of wider communication such as English as an official language while they seek to standardize the indigenous language by means of corpus planning. According to Fishman (1969:113), the decision of A-modal nations to use a language of wider communication as an official language and to promote the Western-style training of an élite are typi-cally justified 'by the basic need to obtain and retain as much tangible aid, as many trained personnel, and as much influence abroad as possible in order to meet the immediate operational demand of nationhood . . . language selection serves *nationism* (i.e. the very operational integrity of the nation).' Many developing nations such as Cameroon, which will be discussed in the 'Case studies' section of this chapter, exemplify this situation.

Uni-modal nations

The second type of language planning context, which Fishman terms *Uni-modal nations,* is characterized by the use of an indigenous language with a literary tradition alongside a language of wider communication which is often left over from a period of colonial rule. Language planning in these countries involves replacing the language of wider communication with an indigenous language as a way of developing a national identity. An example of a Uni-modal nation is Tanzania, where the use of Swahili is replacing English. The following passage on the role of Swahili in Tanzania illustrates quite well the assumptions which underlie language planning in Uni-modal nations.

> A common indigenous language in the modern nation states is a powerful factor for unity. Cutting across tribal and ethnic lines, it promotes a feeling of single community. Additionally it makes possible the expression and development of social ideas, economic targets and cultural identity easily perceived by citizens. It is, in a word, a powerful factor for mobilisation of people and resources for nationhood.
>
> In Tanzania we have been blessed with such a language—Swahili. Whatever the existing variation of dialect and diction, and local mutilation of meanings of given words notwithstanding, Swahili is spoken and understood throughout the length and breadth of the land. Indeed there is a noticeable trend towards designating Africans as Swahilis—though the historical Swahilis are a distinct ethnic and sociological grouping.
>
> Quite obviously this common language is a precious heritage and asset. It can serve a double purpose. Firstly it can reveal the wealth of political, economic and social ideas and values of our past. In so doing, it can reveal part of the historical foundation of Tanzania as a nation. Secondly, it can be the medium of formulating the political, economic and social principles, plans and goals of our nation in this day and age. In so doing it will serve as the other linchpin in the foundation of our identity. (*The Nationalist,* December 20th, 1968 (as cited in Fishman (1969:117))

As is evident from this passage, in Uni-modal nations, the promotion of an indigenous language as the language of wider communication is viewed as essential to the development of a sense of national pride and unity.

However, Uni-modal nations can be faced with a great deal of corpus planning if the language which is chosen as the national language is not standardized and few technical texts have been translated into it.

Multi-modal nations

Finally, in *Multi-modal nations* a number of languages, each with a literary tradition, exist side by side. In such instances, since there is competition among various languages for official recognition, compromises have to be made in designating an official language. According to Fishman, typically in such nations:

> in order to avoid giving any party an advantage—and in order to avoid constant rivalry for greater national prominence among the various contenders—a foreign Language of Wider Communication is frequently selected de jure or utilized de facto as (co-) official or as working language . . . at the national level (sometimes in conjunction with an indigenous national language which may actually be little employed by those who are ostensibly its guardians). (Fishman 1969:121)

Many of these nations promote bilingualism through their language planning. An example of this type of country is India, which has several indigenous languages and has designated both Hindi (an indigenous language) and English (a foreign Language of Wider Communication) as official languages.

Table 1.1 illustrates the difference between the three types of nation in terms of the relative roles of the national language and the language of wider communication.

| | Type of nation | | |
	A-modal	*Uni-modal*	*Multi-modal*
Reasons for selecting a national language	Governed by considerations of political integration (nationism)	Governed by considerations of national identity (nationalism)	Governed by a need to compromise between the demands of competing indigenous languages and political integration

Table 1.1: National languages and the languages of wider communication in the developing nations (adapted from Fishman 1969:112)

In order to illustrate how the issues of nationism and nationalism influence language planning and educational policies, we will examine the situation in three specific countries: Cameroon, Malaysia, and the Philippines. In all three countries English enjoys some official status, yet they differ in the relationship between their indigenous languages and English, with Cameroon exemplifying the characteristics of an A-modal nation, Malaysia those of a Uni-modal nation, and the Philippines those of a Multi-modal nation.

Case studies

A-modal nations: Cameroon

Cameroon is a truly multilingual area: there are 200 to 300 vernaculars; two official languages, French and English; Cameroon Pidgin English, which is a widely used and an unrecognized lingua franca, and a number of African languages of wider communication along with a non-indigenous language, Arabic (Todd 1982:122). The language situation of Cameroon is a good example of an A-modal nation where language decisions were made on the basis of nationism rather than nationalism. In 1919, after a long tradition of European trade and a period of German colonization, Cameroon was ceded to France and Britain as part of the Treaty of Versailles, with four-fifths going to France and one-fifth going to Britain. After this, in the francophone sector, French was the sole medium of instruction and teachers were forbidden to use either the vernacular or Pidgin English (the latter was widely spoken at that time as a result of earlier English missionary schools in the area). In the anglophone sector, although initially vernacular education was supported, by 1960 it had been entirely abandoned and replaced with English-medium schools (Todd 1982:125-6).

In 1960 the francophone sector became independent and a year later, as the result of a plebiscite, the southern part of the anglophone sector was reunited with the francophone sector as the Federal Republic of the Cameroon. One of the first questions facing the new government was the issue of selecting an official language policy. In this case, nationism and expediency were the deciding factors. As Todd points out:

> the new government was anxious to extend education and to estab-
> lish a language policy that would be acceptable to both sections of
> the federated state and of value to the country as a whole. It there-
> fore adopted French and English as the official languages of the state.
> *The selection was based on practical expedience* [my italics]. No single

vernacular could be selected as a language of national unity, and it was neither possible nor desirable to standardise and use all the Cameroonian mother tongues. A bilingual approach was also adopted towards education. From nursery schools upwards all education was to be in either French or English, with bilingualism in these two official languages being encouraged and being specifically catered for in a number of secondary schools and in the university. (Todd 1982:127)

Today, in the francophone sector of Cameroon, where French is the medium of instruction, although it is the official policy to introduce English, the lack of qualified teachers makes this difficult. The main incentive for anyone in this area to learn English is an economic one since throughout the country there are more job opportunities for bilingual –individuals. In the anglophone sector of the country, theoretically English is the medium of instruction. However, the variety of English that is used is one influenced by the existence of the many mother tongues spoken in the area, by French, and by Cameroon Pidgin English. Thus, a major issue in this area is which standard of English should be taught in the schools.

In terms of language teaching, A-modal nations like Cameroon will often exhibit two characteristics. First, it is quite likely that many of the country's teachers will not be very fluent in English. When teachers are not fluent in a language and yet are required to use it as the medium of instruction, they may react in different ways. Some may work hard to gain competency in the language and therefore be eager to attend workshops and in-service training courses. Others may feel so unsure of their English skills that they in fact make little use of the language in their classrooms, even though the country's education policy dictates that they should use it. The second characteristic of many A-modal nations—also true of Multi-modal nations—is that the variety of English spoken throughout the country will be affected by the other languages that are also spoken. Thus, a nativized variety of English with many phonemic, structural, and lexical variations from Standard English may be in general use. We will return to the issue of nativized varieties of English and how it affects the language classroom in Chapter 4.

Uni-modal nations: Malaysia

Malaysia is an example of a Uni-modal nation in which there is an indigenous language, Bahasa Malaysia, with a literary tradition, and a language of wider communication, English, left from an earlier colonial period. Today, Malaysia is composed of three major ethnic groups: Malays who comprise over half of the population, Chinese who make up about thirtysix per cent of the population, and Tamils who make up ten per cent.

British influence in Malaysia began in the early nineteenth century. In the 1890s, the British began investing heavily in Malaya to develop their transportation network and rubber plantations. Because the British paid little attention to educational policy, responsibility for developing schools rested within the various ethnic communities themselves. Between 1942 and 1945, during the Japanese occupation, primary schooling was available in Malay, English, Tamil, and Chinese with each community typically establishing their own schools; secondary education was available in English and Chinese, and higher education only in English (Watson 1983:135). Since the majority of Malays and Tamils did not continue their schooling after primary level, the élite that did continue their education did so in English.

After the Second World War, a rise in Malayan nationalism resulted in independence in 1957. After independence, the new government's attention to educational reform resulted in the setting up of the Razak Commission. This Commission urged the establishment of a national system of education with a common curriculum in which the national language was to be the medium of instruction with English as a compulsory subject. In this way language-in-education planning was used to support the growing feeling of nationalism in the country.

Today, Bahasa Malaysia is the country's official language with English recognized as an important second language. The decision to designate Bahasa Malaysia as the official language in place of English was made out of a desire to develop a national identity. Tungku Abdul Rahman, the first Chief of State of the Federation of Malay States, who became ruler after the declaration of independence from Great Britain, argued that 'it is only right that as a developing nation we should want a language of our own. . . . If the national language is not introduced, our country will be devoid of a unified character' (as cited in Watson 1983:139). In keeping with this desire to develop a national language, the original name for the language, Bahasa Melayu (the language of the Malays) was changed to Bahasa Malaysia (the language of Malaysia) as a way of indicating that it was to become the common language of all ethnic groups in Malaysia (Chitravelu 1985:86). In order to develop Bahasa Malaysia as a national language, the Dewan Bahasa dan Pustaka (Language and Literature Agency) was created to translate scientific words into the language, standardize pronunciation, and develop Malaysian textbooks for use in schools and colleges. A great deal of corpus planning was undertaken to make Bahasa Malaysia a viable vehicle for educational purposes. In addition, a special agency was established to train teachers from various ethnic backgrounds in the language (Watson 1983:140).

From 1970 onward Bahasa Malaysia replaced English as the medium of instruction in primary schools; by 1978 all national secondary education was conducted in Bahasa Malaysia; by 1982 all upper secondary schools, and by 1983 all University education had undergone this change (Watson 1983:142). This policy has not been well received by the ethnic Chinese and Tamil populations who tend not to identify with the national language and view the acquisition of English as a key to economic betterment. For this reason these ethnic groups favour English-medium schools. The friction caused by the use of Bahasa Malaysia in the schools has made language policy a very sensitive issue. In fact, language policy is such a sensitive issue that there is a great deal of pressure to prevent it being discussed in print or in public except by designated government officials (Noss 1986:13). Thus, the government policy of promoting a national identity through its language policies has not resulted in political unity among the various ethnic groups of Malaysia.

These changes in language policy, especially those in relation to education, have affected the role and status of English in Malaysia. Although the national mass-media publishes in English, Chinese, Malay, and Tamil, the use of Malay as a lingua franca is on the increase. Similarly in the business community, since all transactions must be in the national language, the use of English is on the decline (Noss 1986:13). In terms of the status of English, while the majority of the population support the government policy of giving primary status to the national language, a sizeable minority (largely, but not exclusively, ethnic Chinese and Tamils) still prefer the use of English.

Attitudes toward the study of English in countries like Malaysia can differ greatly depending on the ethnic background of the individual. Among those who support the promotion of an indigenous language as a way of achieving a unique national identity, like the Malaysian in Malaysia, the study of English may be viewed as an impediment to the building of nationalism. On the other hand, among those who do not identify with the major ethnic group, as is the case with many of the Chinese and Tamils in Malaysia, the study of English may be valued as promoting a neutral medium of wider communication. The status of English in a country can vary greatly depending on the particular ethnic group involved. However, to the extent that government policies to promote a national language in Unimodal nations are successful, the role of a language of wider communication such as English in such countries will be on the decrease, restricted to use in fewer and fewer domains; hence, students of English are likely to find fewer and fewer occasions on which to use the language.

Multi-modal nations: The Philippines

In a Multi-modal nation, since several languages with a literary tradition exist, compromises have to be made in designating an official language. The Philippines is a good example.

Estimates of the number of languages spoken in the Philippines range between seventy and eighty; however, eight of them have been designated as major languages since they are spoken by the eight largest ethnic groups (Galang 1988:234). In addition, because of colonization, Spanish is spoken by about three per cent of the population and English is widely used. After the United States took over the Philippines in 1898, English became a common medium of communication and instruction and in 1919 it was made the official language for use in the local government and legal system (Galang 1988:23). In the 1930s a movement surfaced to develop a national language as a way of promoting a national identity; this resulted in corpus planning to develop a national language based on Tagalog, which was termed Pilipino. Today, Pilipino and English are the co-official languages.

Countries like the Philippines which have two or more co-official languages tend to use each language in separate domains. In this way they resemble many A-modal nations, like Cameroon, in which the indigenous language is used in some domains, typically the more familiar, and English in other domains, typically the more formal. In the case of the Philippines, English is the primary language for such things as government employment, college admission tests, and computer-related businesses (Sibayan 1985:2). Since English is used primarily in formal contexts with the mother tongue or Pilipino serving more informal contexts, most Filipinos have mastered formal rather than informal English. In fact, Gonzalez (1982:216) contends that it is the rare Filipino who has mastered informal English. What this suggests for language teachers in countries like the Philippines is that students may not be familiar with informal English nor have any need to use it. This is an important fact to consider in designing communicative activities and in selecting texts. Texts which contain dialogues with informal English and require a good deal of role playing based on informal situations are not likely to meet the needs of Filipino students, who tend to use their mother tongue rather than English in such contexts.

Since many well-educated Filipinos are fluent in formal English and in formal and informal Pilipino, one finds in the Philippines a good deal of *code-switching* (shifting from the use of one language to another within a conversation). This style has been termed Taglish (if Tagalog predominates) or Engalog (if English predominates) (Gonzalez 1982:214). It is often used in the mass media to 'establish an atmosphere of informality, perhaps unconsciously excluding a native speaker of English who is familiar with only one code and likewise perhaps unconsciously establishing one's credentials as a nationalist, albeit Westernized' (Gonzalez 1982:217). Code-switching necessitates a high degree of fluency in two languages and can be used, as Gonzalez points out, to establish identity and rapport with other members of the community.

Currently in the Philippines, as in other countries in a post-colonial era, there is a strong movement to replace English with the national language, as was done in Malaysia, in order to develop a national identity. In fact, Sibayan (1985:1-2) in his research on the current status and role of English in the Philippines, concludes 'that Pilipino has taken over in many of the domains that used to be the domain of English . . . [and] that this development is apparently a manifestation of the resurgence of nationalism and the cultural search for identity among Filipinos.' If this movement is successful in the Philippines, English will play an increasingly restricted role.

One factor, however, that may restrict the use of Pilipino in the educational structure of the country is the lack of available reading materials. The Philippines currently has a policy of bilingual education in which both English and Pilipino are used as the media of instruction in elementary and secondary schools. As was pointed out in the beginning of the chapter, in order for a language to be used as a medium of instruction, basic teaching and reading materials must be available in it. Presently such materials are not available in Pilipino. In fact, Sibayan (ibid.:55), in a survey of books and supplementary materials for sale in one of the major textbook distributors in the Manila area, found that overall only nine per cent of the elementary, secondary, and college texts for sale were in Pilipino with only two per cent of all college texts printed in Pilipino. Sibayan contends that one of the most important reasons for the lack of available college texts in Pilipino 'is that Pilipino is not yet fully intellectualized for use in most learned subjects' (ibid.:55). If Pilipino is eventually to assume the importance that government officials wish it to have in society, a good deal of corpus planning will be necessary so that complex ideas in specialized fields of learning can be expressed in the language.

Conclusion

The role and status of English in a country is closely related to language-planning decisions. In A-modal nations, the use of English as a language of wider communication is encouraged throughout society; in addition, since English is typically the medium of instruction and the key to becoming a member of the educated élite, students are often anxious to learn it. In contrast, in Uni-modal nations, since the ultimate aim is to achieve a monolingual society, the role—and eventually the status—of English will be on the decline. Finally, in Multi-modal nations, which seek to promote a bilingual society, English will most likely be used in certain domains, often more formal ones, with the indigenous language used in more informal contexts. In contrast to the case of Uni-modal nations, the use of English will have status since the language is needed to obtain advancement in the political, economic, and educational communities.

Language policies, by specifying the choice of a national language and the medium of instruction, determine who learns English and for what purposes. In addition, language policies, by promoting or restricting the use of English within a country, can influence social attitudes toward the use of English, as was illustrated in the case of Malaysia. While it is important for expatriate language teachers to recognize the impact that the social and political structure has on their job, it is equally important for them to recognize that it is not their function to change such policies. As Abbott (1984:98) points out, 'the establishment of a role for English in any country is part of that country's educational policy, and is quite rightly effected with little or no reference to outside expertise; expatriates who hold advisory positions soon become aware of how seldom their advice is sought, let alone heeded.' Thus, teachers abroad will have little opportunity and indeed little right to attempt to change the ways English is taught and used in the country. Rather, their primary role will be to teach English as effectively as they can within the existing social and political context.

In this chapter we have seen how the social and political structure of a country affects language teaching. Language policies rest in the hands of politicians, and even when language-planning issues are delegated to language specialists, their decision will be reviewed by politicians who make polices on the basis of political criteria. To politicians, one important consideration in language planning is the issue of nationism versus nationalism. The choice as to which of these is given more weight will be reflected in the country's language policies. While the role and status of English in a country is clearly affected by the social and political structure, this is not the only factor which will influence its use. Equally important is the economic context of a country, which can either promote or undermine the spread of English. It is this influence that we turn to in Chapter 2.

Exploring the ideas

1 As was pointed out at the beginning of the chapter, teaching English is an activity infused with social and political significance. Judd (1987:15-16), in his article on the teaching of English as a political act, points out that various moral dilemmas can arise from teaching English in an international context.

   First, in some instances the teaching of English may be contributing to the loss of another language, as can happen in A-modal nations where the use of English as the official language is encouraged in place of developing the use of an indigenous language. Judd asks: 'Should we be concerned about this state of affairs?'

Second, in some countries the learning of English is accessible only to the élite, as was the case in Malaysian higher education before the change in language policy was enacted, thus helping to perpetuate the established power structure. Judd asks: 'Should we question the motives of our students or accept unquestioningly the determination of who is to study English and who is not?'

Third, in some areas English is a vehicle for personal advancement, yet because the competition for good jobs is so severe, knowledge of English is not sufficient to obtain top jobs. Often advancement is based on political connections rather than the ability to speak English. Judd asks: 'Should we participate in an educational process which nurtures illusion?'

Discuss your reaction to each of the dilemmas posed by Judd. What do you think expatriate teachers can and should do to alter language policies that they believe result in undesirable social consequences? Since the role of expatriate teachers is not to change official language policies, what might language teachers do on an interpersonal level to affect policies such as those listed above?

2 Myanmar (formerly Burma) was a British colony from 1885 to 1947. The following is an excerpt from the British Council English Language Teaching Profile on Myanmar (1981:1) regarding the present role of English in the country.

> In the 'colonial' period (the nineteenth century to 1947) everyone with any pretensions to education wanted to learn English as the key to a safe job in the Government service—chiefly in missionary schools, where the medium of instruction was English, and in Anglo-vernacular schools, where it was a subject in the lower classes and medium in the higher. After the war, Burmese became the medium of instruction, but, almost inevitably, English continued to be widely used and taught until 1962. In the succeeding three years, all missionary and other private schools were nationalized, and a campaign for 'Burmese in Burma' was pursued.

Based on this description of the role of English in Myanmar, how would you characterize Myanmar, as an A-modal, Uni-modal, or Multi-modal nation? How has the country used language-in-education planning decisions to support the development of nationalism? What problems may Mynamar be faced with in terms of corpus planning to utilize Burmese as the medium of instruction?

3 English and Sesotho are the official languages of Lesotho. The following is an excerpt from the British Council English Language Teaching Profile (1979:1) on the present role of English in Lesotho.

Sesotho is the first language of almost all Basotho [the largest ethnic group in Lesotho], though there are small groups of Xhosa and Nguni speakers in the Kingdom. Lesotho was under British protection and administration for nearly a century. It remains a member of the Commonwealth and has strong political links with other former British possessions in Africa. Economically it is very dependent on South Africa, and a large proportion of Basotho males spend much of their working lives as contract workers in the mines of South Africa. English is therefore widely understood and used. It is the medium of communication in Government, the High Courts, and business, and is the alternative language of the National Assembly. Lesotho also receives large amounts of technical assistance from overseas and is popular with tourists from South Africa, both of which facts contribute further to the use of English among urban Basotho.

The school system in Lesotho is based on 7 years of primary education (in Standards 1-7) followed by secondary education for 5 years. . . . According to the government syllabus, the aim is 'to equip the child with a knowledge of English adequate to enable him to understand and appreciate the spoken language'. Pupils are to receive such a thorough grounding in both spoken and written English that they will encounter 'no great hardship in using English as a medium of instruc- tion' in secondary schools or training colleges. Up to Standard 3, English is taught as a subject. In Standard 4, it 'should be increasingly introduced whenever possible. From Standard 5 upwards English should be the sole medium of instruction, Sesotho only being resorted to for explanation of difficulties'.

Based on this description of the role of English in Lesotho, how would you characterize Lesotho, as an A-modal, Uni-modal, or Multi-modal nation? How has the country used language-in-education planning decisions to support the development of nationism? What difficulties might the government encounter in promoting its language-in-educa- tion policy in terms of teacher fluency and determining a standard of English usage?

4 Language planning necessitates choices. Often the choice of an official language or languages is based on compromise. One country that will face difficult language-planning questions is a post-apartheid South Africa. The following is some information about the linguistic situation in South Africa.

Today South Africa has a population of approximately 30 million people who speak the following languages:

1. Previously, approximately five million people were designated as

White—three million of which are native English speakers and two million native Afrikaans speakers.

2. There were one million people who were designated as Indian. Of these one million, almost all, except for a few Hindi speakers, are native English speakers.

3. South Africa has approximately three million individuals who were designated as Colored. Of these, eighty percent are native Afrikaans speakers and twenty percent are native English speakers.

4. The remaining twenty-one million people were designated as African. Of these, six million are Zulu speakers and four million are native Xhosa speakers. The remaining eleven million Africans speak a variety of African languages. Those Africans who attend school have been exposed to English since English is the medium of instruction in the schools from fifth grade on. However, rural Africans, who have had little formal education, are more familiar with Afrikaans since they interact more commonly with Afrikaans speakers.

In reference to language attitudes the following is important.

1. White Afrikaans speakers hold most of the political power and are committed to preserving the Afrikaans language.

2. Many individuals who were designated as Colored cherish Afrikaans since it is their native language; however, for some Coloreds, Afrikaans is viewed as the language of the oppressor and thus, they would prefer to use English.

3. Many Africans, although they wish to maintain their native language, view the acquisition of Afrikaans and English as a necessary condition for social and economic betterment. Currently some black consciousness groups are stressing the need for Whites to learn African languages.

(Source of Demographics: *Encyclopedia Britannica, 1989 Book of the Year*, and *Official Yearbook of the Republic of South Africa, 1986*.)

If South Africa were to promote nationism over nationalism to foster political unity and economic expediency, what language policy do you think it might enact regarding an official language or languages? What language-in-education policy do you think the country might adopt in terms of a medium of instruction in order to promote nationism?

If South Africa were to promote nationalism over nationism, what language policy do you think it might enact? What indigenous language or languages might be chosen to replace colonial languages as a way of developing a national identity? What language-in-education policy do you think South Africa might enact in terms of the medium of instruction? What corpus planning might need to be undertaken?

Researching the ideas

1 Research the role and status of English in a country in which you might be interested in teaching and characterize it according to the A-modal, Uni-modal, Multi-modal distinction. Describe both the historical and current role of English in the country and discuss how language-in-education policies have been used to support the development of nationalism or nationism. In addition, describe any corpus planning that the country has undertaken to support its status planning decisions.

You might begin your research by checking to see if a British Council English Language Teaching Profile exists on the country. The British Council has compiled English teaching profiles on many countries; these profiles include a section on the overall status and role of English in the country, as well as an in-depth analysis of the role of English in the educational structure of the country. These profiles are available through ERIC (the Educational Resource Information Center) which can be obtained in most academic libraries.

2 Research the corpus planning process of a country which is involved in what Cooper (1983) calls *elaboration* or modernization of the language such as is being undertaken for Swahili in Tanzania. Elaboration involves modifying a language so that it can be used for a new function like expressing technical or scientific concepts. Presently language planning agencies for Arabic, Pilipino, Swahili, and Hindi all exist to produce and disseminate new scientific and technical terminology in the language. The following are some sources listed by Cooper (1983) on this topic:

Alishjahbana, S.T. 1971. 'Language policy, language engineering and literacy in Indonesia and Malaysia' in *Current Trends in Linguistics* 8:1025-38.

Altoma, S.J. 1970. 'Language education in Arab countries and the role of the academies' in *Current Trends in Linguistics* 6:690-720.

Fellman, J. 1974. 'The Academy of the Hebrew language: its history, structure and function' in *International Journal of the Sociology of Language* 1:95-103.

Sibayan, B.P. 1971. 'Language policy, language engineering and literacy: the Philippines' in *Current Trends in Linguistics* 8:1038-62.

Other references for this project are the books by Cooper (1989) and Fishman (1974) listed in the 'Suggestions for further reading'.

Suggestions for further reading

Cooper, R.L. 1989. *Language Planning and Social Change.* Cambridge: Cambridge University Press.
This book provides a general overview of language planning with specific chapters on status planning and corpus planning. Language planning is related to public policy and social change.

Eastman, C. 1983. *Language Planning: An Introduction.* San Francisco, Calif.: Chandler and Sharp Publishers.
This book provides a general introduction to the field of language planning. The book contains a history of the subject, as well as chapters on language-planning theory and methods. The relationship between language planning and social science, politics, economics, anthropology, and education is also examined.

Fishman, J. (ed.) 1974. *Advances in Language Planning.* The Hague: Mouton.
This book is a collection of essays on language-planning studies in Turkey, Sub-Saharan Africa, New Guinea, Australia, the Philippines, French Polynesia, Israel, and Canada. Of particular interest in terms of the issue of a standardized language variety are the articles on the role of academies and standardization efforts in Arabic countries, Latin America, Sub-Saharan Africa, Indonesia, Malaysia, Israel, and China.

Kennedy, C. (ed.) 1983. *Language Planning and Language Education.* London: George Allen and Unwin.
This is a collection of readings containing articles on language-planning survey results, evaluation procedures, and case studies on language planning and education. Specific studies are included on the situation in the Philippines, Kenya, Malaysia, Cameroon, and Sweden.

Rubin, J. and **B.H. Jernudd** (eds.) 1971. *Can Language be Planned?* Honolulu, HI: The University Press of Hawaii.
This book contains papers on language planning presented by scholars from various disciplines at a meeting at the East-West Center in Hawaii. The conference stressed the need for a multidisciplinary approach to language planning. The papers deal with research strategies and general approaches to the subject. Included in the collection are case studies on language planning in Ireland, Israel, the Philippines, Turkey, Malaysia, Pakistan, and Eastern Africa.

Rubin, J., B.H. Jernudd, J. Das Gupta, J. Fishman, and **C. Ferguson** (eds.) 1977. *Language Planning Processes.* The Hague: Mouton.
This is a seminal collection of articles containing case studies on the language-planning processes of India, Israel, Indonesia, Sweden, and China. Also included is an article by Rubin on the manner in which text-book writers in Israel and Indonesia approached language-planning issues.

2 LANGUAGE TEACHING AND THE ECONOMIC CONTEXT

Theoretical background

Cooper and Seckbach (1977) maintain that economic rewards are important incentives for motivating an individual to learn a language. They contend that

> Lingua francas, for example, often spread along trade routes and radiate from market centers, carried by traders who need a common language in order to do business. In colonial territories, the language of the imperial administration often spreads in part because proficiency in the language becomes a prerequisite for government employment and school attendance. . . .When knowledge of a language becomes associated with material benefits, and when people have the opportunity to learn it, they are likely to do so. (Cooper and Seckbach 1977:212)

This chapter explores how the economic structure of a country, by providing material benefits for knowing English, affects English language teaching. To begin, we examine the following question: How are economic incentives related to individual reasons for learning English, to the spread of English throughout the world, and to the situations in which English is used in particular countries? In the second part of the chapter, the case studies discuss what economic rewards exist in specific countries to encourage the acquisition of English. Throughout the chapter we examine how economic incentives to learn English affect language teaching.

Motivation and attitudes

Integrative versus instrumental motivation

Based on their study of foreign language learners in Canada, Gardner and Lambert (1972) made a distinction between *integrative* and *instrumental* motivation. According to Gardner and Lambert, an individual is integratively motivated when he or she wants to learn another language 'to learn more about the cultural community, because he is interested in it in an open-minded way to the point of eventually being accepted as a member of that group' (ibid. 1972:3). On the other hand, an individual is instrumentally motivated when he or she wants to learn another language for the social benefits or economic rewards this knowledge brings such as getting a job or passing a university entrance examination.

Initial research by Lambert (1972) found a high correlation between integrative motivation and high language proficiency test scores among learners of French in Canada. Subsequent research done by Lukmani (1972) among non-westernized Indian students studying English in Bombay found a high correlation between instrumental motivation and high test scores. These contradictory findings suggest that motivational factors need to be assessed within the larger social context. It may be that in countries where English is not widely used, even in Uni-modal nations where the use of English is restricted, the economic rewards for knowing English in the society are great enough to provide an important source of instrumental motivation.

Intrinsic and extrinsic sources of motivation

Bailey (1986) further distinguishes integrative and instrumental motivation according to whether or not the motivation stems from intrinsic or extrinsic sources. Table 2.1 clarifies this added distinction.

	Intrinsic	Extrinsic
Integrative	Learner wishes to integrate with the L2 culture (e.g. for immigration or marriage)	Someone else wishes the learner to know the L2 for integrative reasons (e.g. Japanese parents send kids to Japanese-language school)
Instrumental	Learner wishes to achieve goals utilizing L2 (e.g. for a career)	External power wants learner to learn L2 (e.g. corporation sends Japanese businessman to US for language training)

Table 2.1: Integrative and instrumental motivation contrasted by intrinsic and extrinsic source (Bailey 1986, as cited in Brown 1987:117)

The economic benefits of learning English provide an important source of instrumental motivation. Such economic benefits can stem from either intrinsic or extrinsic sources. When the motivation arises from intrinsic sources, individuals desire to learn English because they believe this will lead to a better job or some other type of economic benefit. When the motivation arises from an extrinsic source, an employer actually provides economic incentives to learn English. Intrinsically derived instrumental motivation is based on an individual's belief that economic rewards will accrue from learning English, while extrinsically motivated instrumental motivation is based on actual economic benefits given an individual by a corporation or government.

Investigating an individual's reasons for studying English provides an indication of whether or not that person has intrinsic instrumental motivation to learn English centering on the goal of economic betterment. If individuals have this type of motivation, they are likely to give economic benefits as their main incentive for learning English. On the other hand, investigating whether or not businesses or governments in a country actually pay more to individuals who are proficient in English provides an indication of whether or not extrinsic sources of instrumental motivation exist there.

The case studies at the end of the chapter examine to what extent people who are studying English in non-anglophone countries list economic reasons for doing so; in addition, they explore whether or not economic rewards for learning the language actually exist in the country concerned. The surveys discussed in the case studies ask participants to list their reasons for learning English, thus providing insight into an individual's motives. Such questions, however, do not provide an adequate view of an individual's attitude toward English.

Attitudes toward English

As Fishman (1977b:302) points out, the fact that an individual knows English and uses it does not demonstrate that he or she likes the language. In fact, in his study of the relationship between language competence, use, and attitudes of high school and university teachers and students in India, Indonesia, and Israel Fishman found that the relationship between linguistic competence and attitudes toward English is a complex one. In this study, the best attitudinal predictor of English competence was whether an individual's view of life took in modern developments or was based entirely on local traditions. In addition, the study showed a negative correlation between language competence and positive views toward a national language or a sense of nationalism, suggesting that in Uni-modal countries like Malaysia, where strong national sentiments exist supporting the use of the national language, individuals who hold such attitudes are less likely to be competent in English. On the basis of his study, Fishman contends that

> English may be expected to continue as the language of technology in Third World settings for as long as politically low-keyed Anglo-

American domination in this domain continues. Attitudinal resistance to English in this respect can be expected to weaken as
younger generations successively shed more and more of the puristic
and exclusivistic ideologies that their parents and teachers formu-
lated and espoused during the formative struggles for political and
cultural independence. Acquisition and use of English should
increase as educational opportunity becomes decreasingly dependent
on social advantage and as modernization orientations reach successively larger population segments in the Third World. On the whole,
there is no likelihood of mother tongue replacement by English.
Rather, increased acquisition and use of and improved attitudes
toward English as an additional language are likely, particularly in
technological contexts. (Fishman 1977b:308-9)

Fishman's prediction that there will be increased acquisition of English,
particularly in technological contexts, has important implications for
language teaching. It suggests that in countries where English is used
primarily for scientific purposes there will be a demand for courses which
focus on English for Science and Technology. Fishman's optimism that the
language will continue to spread is contingent on opportunities to learn
English becoming less dependent on individual economic wealth, and on
modernization reaching more people. Let us then examine what is meant
by *language spread* and what other factors may foster the spread of
English.

Language spread

Influence of former colonial powers

Cooper (1982:6) defines language spread as 'an increase, over time, in the
proportion of a communication network that adopts a given language or
language variety for a given communicative purpose.' Today, many countries have adopted English as a language of wider communication making
it a world lingua franca. Conrad and Fishman (1977:6) point out that
today English 'is *the* language of diplomacy, the predominant language in
which mail is written, the principal language of aviation and of radio
broadcasting, the first language of nearly 300 million people, and an
additional language of perhaps that many more.' One important impetus
for the spread of English has been the imperialism of English-speaking
countries. In fact, almost all of the countries which now include English
as one of their official or semi-official languages were at one time former
colonies of the United States or Britain. The following list, showing
countries which give English some official function, demonstrates this
fact.

Non-English mother-tongue countries where English has official functions:

Bangladesh	Israel	Nauru	Sudan
Botswana	Kenya	Nigeria	Swaziland
Brunei	Lesotho	Pakistan	Tanzania
Cameroon	Liberia	Philippines	Tonga
Ethiopia	Malawi	Seychelles	Uganda
Fiji	Malaysia	Sierra Leone	Western Samoa
Gambia	Malta	Singapore	Zambia
Ghana	Mauritius	South Africa	Zimbabwe
India	Namibia	Sri Lanka	

(Source: Lowenberg 1989:216)

Today, however, in a post-colonial era, English is continuing to spread both in countries where it has been afforded official status and in countries where it has no official status. Indeed, English is still being used even in Uni-modal countries like Malaysia where it has been replaced as the official language by Bahasa Malaysia. The question is why: clearly, individuals and societies must have a reason for adopting a second language. As Fishman says

> languages are rarely acquired for their own sake. They are acquired as keys to other things that are desired. We must first identify and document what these are, if only because such documentation will help us explain why, how and among whom English as an additional language is or is not spreading. (Fishman 1977a:115)

According to Fishman, in order for one language, such as English, to spread and ultimately replace another language, there must be some belief that the shift will result in access to scarce power and resources.

The linguistic power of English

Kachru argues persuasively that one central reason for the spread of English is the widespread belief that proficiency in English can transmute an individual or a speech community by providing

> an added potential for material and social gain and advantage. . . . In comparison with other languages of wider communication, knowing English is like possessing the fabled Aladdin's lamp, which permits one to open, as it were, the linguistic gates to international business, technology, science, and travel. In short, English provides linguistic power. (Kachru 1986:1)

Regardless of whether or not proficiency in English does result in greater economic and social gains, the belief that it can do this provides an important incentive for individuals to learn it.

The current situation in South Africa provides a good context for illustrating some of the factors that are contributing to the spread of English. Presently most citizens of South Africa speak an indigenous language at home and in informal settings; however, either English or Afrikaans, as the official languages of the country, are employed in the majority of formal settings. While today Afrikaans is used by more black South Africans at work than English, Meerkotter, a white South African, predicts that English will become the lingua franca in South Africa. He gives two reasons why he believes this will occur: first, Afrikaans for many South Africans is a symbol of oppression while English has fewer of these negative associations, and second, English is viewed as the language of education, the source of information and mobility. He maintains that

> more people are willing to learn and speak English than Afrikaans because the latter tongue is associated largely with an establishment which is not perceived as a symbol representing an open, free and united democratic country. The status of English as an educational, social, and political instrument for communication is also such that it outweighs the positive features of the other languages. (Meerkotter 1987:141)

Meerkotter's prediction concerning the role of English in South Africa is based on the assumption that two elements promote the spread of a language: first, a positive attitude toward it, and second, social, educational, and political incentives for learning it. In many countries of the world today English scores high on both counts. Although in some countries English is negatively associated with an era of colonialism, as it becomes more and more of an international language used in various business and scientific areas, it may well lose these negative associations. Thus, proficiency in English may be desired more because it is the language of business, science, and technology than because it is the language of any one culture.

Tunisia is another country which illustrates reasons why the use of English is continuing to spread. In Tunisia, unlike South Africa, English has no official status: Arabic is the official language and French is widely spoken as a result of former French colonization. While the use of French in some areas of public life is striking and a knowledge of French is still considered to be a prerequisite for a well-paid job, Salhi (1984:192-3), in his study of the role of English in Tunisia, contends that English is still of considerable importance. According to Salhi (ibid.:188), since English rather than French is necessary for advanced studies in specialized fields of science and technology, it is needed so that the country will have a 'true language of wider communication', allowing Tunisians to interact in the international science and business community. While Salhi (ibid.:192-3) is committed to the use of Arabic as the official language and the medium of instruction at all levels, he believes that English, particularly at the university level in specialized fields, needs to be encouraged. He believes that the use of English in Tunisia 'should be viewed as a window on the entire world and not just the Anglo-American nations, and the instrument of science and technology as long as these terms are synonymous with development and modernization.' Salhi, then, foresees a particular role for English in Tunisia, mainly as a language of commerce, science, and technology. To the extent that English does assume this role, English teaching there, as in many countries where the language has a restricted role, will need to focus on English for Specific Purposes.

Economic support for language teaching

The spread of English is affected both by an individual's belief in the value of knowing the language for economic and educational betterment and by actual social and economic rewards. Both of these factors are important in providing economic incentives for learning English. In addition, the spread of English can be either enhanced or restricted by the actual amount of money that a government allocates to teaching it. In this way, economic constraints influence the spread of English.

Countries vary greatly in the amount of their budget devoted to education and this in turn affects the extent and quality of English teaching. Clearly, the more students who are able to have English instruction, the more English will spread. In addition, the better the quality of teaching, the more likely students are to become proficient in English and thus be able to use the language in society. A comparison of English teaching in Guatemala, Honduras, and Costa Rica vividly demonstrates this fact. While Guatemala spends only 1.7 per cent of its budget on education, the lowest in Central America, and Honduras spends 3.5 per cent, Costa Rica spends over a third of its budget on education (Crandall, Miller, Spohnholz, and Wederspahn 1985). Because of this fact, the quality and extent of English teaching in these three countries differs greatly.

In Guatemala, English is required by the Ministry of Education in Grades Seven through Eleven. Yet the instruction is quite poor. Crandall *et al.* in their assessment of English teaching in Central America, make the following generalization about English teaching in Guatemalan public schools:

> The English offered in the public schools is minimal. Eleventh grade graduates could be expected to understand little beyond 'What is your name?', to read only a few isolated English words and to speak no English in spite of having received over 500 hours of English instruction during their secondary schooling. For the most part,

teachers have no formal preparation, classes average 40–to–50 students, and few or totally inadequate textbooks and no visual aids or supporting materials are provided. . . . Although the Ministry of Education has strict requirements that all public secondary school teachers must be certified, only a very small percentage of persons teaching English in the government's *basico* program are actually certified in the area of English instruction. (Crandall *et al.* 1985:20–1)

While the quality of instruction in the best private schools in Guatemala is better than that of the public schools, many of the teachers in these schools are also untrained.

A similar situation exists in Honduras where 'the quality of English language instruction in urban public schools is substandard' with the English teacher having little or no pedagogical training (ibid.:36). In addition, vast differences exist between the quality of education in urban and rural schools, with many rural secondary schools not even offering the required foreign language. The best instruction in English in Honduras exists in private language and bilingual schools. In fact, 'interest in English is so keen among wealthy Hondurans that they will register their children for certain private English language schools at birth to assure them of the few coveted places (ibid.:35). Thus, the ability to learn English in Honduras, as in many countries, is related not only to the money that the country allocates to the teaching of English but also to individual wealth.

The English teaching situation in Costa Rica, where over a third of the budget is devoted to education, differs dramatically from the situation in Guatemala and Honduras. Costa Rica, 'to a greater extent than many Latin American nations, actually follows its published educational designs, even in the rural schools. Indeed there is less difference in the quality of public education between urban and rural schools in Costa Rica than is found elsewhere' (ibid.:67). Because of this fact, graduating secondary public schools students in Costa Rica will tend to be more proficient in English than comparable students in Guatemala or Honduras, which may well be one significant reason why English is spreading in Costa Rica. In fact, Crandall *et al.* (ibid.:66) maintain that, in Costa Rica, English 'while enjoying no official status on a national level, is rapidly becoming the expected second language in business, professional and governmental circles.' In Costa Rica then, as in Tunisia, even though the government through its national policies has afforded no official status to English, the language is assuming an important but restricted role in the country. In countries like Costa Rica and Tunisia where English is used in restricted domains, the demand for English for Specific Purposes courses may be quite high.

The spread of English, then, is closely related to individual belief in the economic value of English, that is, to the actual economic benefits afforded by a society for knowing the language, and by the amount of money allocated for teaching it. Another reason for the spread of English involves the domains in which it is used in a country, often more formal ones related to economic structure. When, in multilingual nations, English is the predominant language used in domains in which many white-collar jobs exist such as business, the mass media, education, and government, then individuals want to know English to get these jobs. The idea of specific domains in a multilingual nation being dominated by a particular language is referred to as diglossia.

Diglossia

The term *diglossia* was first introduced by Ferguson in 1959 in reference to a situation in which a society uses two varieties of a language, each with clearly defined roles. While Ferguson restricted his definition to two *varieties* of the same language, Fishman (1972) expanded Ferguson's concept of diglossia to include the separate use of two distinct *languages* within a society. Diglossia is not the same as bilingualism. Whereas bilingualism 'refers to an individual's ability to use more than one language variety,' diglossia 'refers to the distribution of more than one language variety to serve different communicational tasks in a society' (Fasold 1984:40). For a society to be classified as having both bilingualism and diglossia, almost everyone in the society needs to know both varieties or languages used by the society. A-modal nations, to the extent that they encourage the use of indigenous languages, and Multi-modal nations, to the extent that their bilingual policy is effective, will have societal bilingualism. However, they will not exhibit diglossia unless the two languages serve different functions in the society.

Central to the concept of diglossia is the idea that one of the two languages or varieties has more prestige than the other and is, in Ferguson's (1959) terms, the High variety (or H) while the other variety, the Low variety (or L), is afforded much less prestige. According to Ferguson, specific functions tend to occur with each variety. The High variety or language tends to be used in formal contexts like government, business, education, and commerce, domains in which white-collar jobs exist, while the Low variety tends to be used in informal contexts for talking with family, friends, and lower status workers (Fasold 1984:52). Table 2.2 (overleaf) demonstrates typical situations where each variety is used.

In many A-modal and Multi-modal countries today where English has official or co-official status, for example India or the Philippines, English is used in domains associated with a High variety, domains that are closely linked to the economic structure of the country. A study by Sridhar

(1982) on language use in India demonstrates how English is preferred in more formal domains. In his study, Sridhar questioned 299 students and 88 employees in Bangalore and Shimoga regarding the domains in which they used their mother tongue, Hindi or Urdu, and English. Within formal and utilitarian domains like speaking to teachers, to strangers on the bus, or to office and bank employees, students reported that they preferred using English over their mother tongue, or Hindi or Urdu. However, the mother tongue was preferred in intimate and affective domains such as talking with family and friends.

Situation	Variety	
	H	L
Sermon in church or mosque	x	
Instructions to servants, waiters, workmen, clerks		x
Personal letter	x	
Speech in parliament, political speech	x	
University lecture	x	
Conversation with family, friends, colleagues		x
News broadcasts	x	
Radio 'soap opera'		x
Newspaper editorial, news story, caption, or picture	x	
Caption on political cartoon		x
Poetry	x	
Folk literature		x

Table 2.2: Typical situations and choices of H or L in diglossia (Ferguson 1959)

In terms of the domains in which the employees used English, Sridhar again found a clear preference for the mother tongue in intimate domains with a preference for English in business contexts in their interactions with colleagues and superiors, and with customers who did not share the same mother tongue. The one exception to using English in business contexts was when employees spoke with subordinates where they preferred to use the mother tongue, or Hindi or Urdu. This in itself indicates the prestige associated with the use of English. The study illustrates how English in India is used in more formal contexts, particularly in those related to the economic structure of the country. It suggests that in India, in order to operate effectively in business transactions, one needs to know English. The need to know English for business transactions rather than for interactions with family and friends may well be one reason for Lukmani's (1972) findings, cited on page 26, regarding the high correlation in India between instrumental motivation and high test scores.

The case studies which follow examine two countries in terms of the following questions. First, what reasons do people in the country have for learning English? Are they related to a belief in the economic benefits of knowing English? Second, is English spreading within the country? Is this growth, if it exists, due to actual economic benefits that exist in the job market for knowing English? And finally, how is English being used within the country? Is it being used in domains associated with a High variety that tend to promote economic mobility? The two countries we will investigate are Thailand, a Uni-modal country in which English has no official status, and the Philippines, a Multi-modal country in which English is a co-official language.

Case studies

Thailand

Thailand has only one official language, Standard or Central Thai, which is used for all communication purposes. English has no particular status in the country; officially it is considered to have equal status with other foreign languages. In reality, however, it has a very special role. According to Sukwiwat (1985:64), 'more than a century ago, English was needed for national survival, today it is needed for economic survival. As stated by one of the prominent educators in the country, Dr. Sippanond Ketuda, "English is no longer a matter of preference. It is a matter of necessity." ' Thailand, like many other southeast Asian countries, is experiencing a rapid increase in the use of English. It is by far the most popular foreign language in the secondary schools and universities; it is also a compulsory subject in all vocational education. Furthermore, English classes are offered at a growing number of private institutions outside of the public educational system (Sukwiwat 1985:9-20).

Why are Thais choosing to study English? In order to answer this question, Shaw (1983) interviewed 313 final year bachelor's degree students in the fields of English language and literature, engineering, and business as to their reasons for studying English. He found that the two main reasons listed were: (1) so that they could talk to native speakers of English and other foreigners for business/educational reasons, and (2) because they believed they would need English for their work. In another survey, Sukwiwat (1985:49) questioned 212 Thai language teachers as to their reasons for studying English. The most important reason given by this group was because they found it useful to their present job. Sukwiwat (ibid.:50) also surveyed 42 key individuals in the educational system, the media, government, and the business community, asking them to list what they believed were the three most important reasons for studying English. The two most popular reasons given were: (1) to acquire advanced knowledge, and (2) to get a good job. Thus, these surveys suggest that the primary reasons for studying English in Thailand today are instrumental in nature, closely related to present and future career goals.

Many Thais seem to believe that English is important for job purposes, but does their belief reflect the reality of the job market? Does knowing English actually help in getting a job? In order to determine whether or not English is a necessary skill for job opportunities in Thailand, Sukwiwat (ibid.:30-1) examined the classified advertisements from a leading Thai newspaper, *Ban Muan*, and two English newspapers, *The Bangkok Post* and *The National Review*. A total of 419 advertisements from the three newspapers were analyzed over a one-month period. Sukwiwat found that 89.5 per cent of all jobs listed in these newspapers required competence in English. The jobs most frequently requiring English tended to be high-paying ones such as managers, supervisors, engineers, and accountants. Only a few blue-collar jobs like housekeeper or driver required English. Thus, not only does English appear to be an important skill for employment in Thailand, it is even more important for white-collar jobs.

Skill in English is also essential to Thais seeking overseas jobs, especially since they are competing with individuals from countries where English is more widely spoken. While the number of Thais seeking employment overseas is growing at an annual rate of six per cent a year, many of these applicants are not obtaining jobs because of their poor command of English, especially in comparison with Indians, Pakistanis, and Filipinos (*Bangkok Post*, June 30, l985 as cited in Sukwiwat, ibid.:32). Thus, in both the domestic and international job market, 'English is one of the most important qualifications for successful job hunters.'

In addition to job mobility, another important factor that appears to be affecting the spread of English in Thailand is the fact that a good deal of information is accessible to Thais only in English. Sukwiwat (ibid.:34) in a survey of 42 key academics, policy-makers, business people, and media people found that her informants all viewed journals in English as the most significant source of information for them to keep abreast of the latest research findings in their own fields. The respondents also felt that the English language mass media in Thailand provided an important source of international and financial news, not available to them in Thai.

The results of the studies cited above suggest that several factors may be contributing to the spread of English in Thailand. First, many Thais appear to view the acquisition of English as important to their present and future career goals, particularly for access to high-paying jobs. Thus, intrinsic instrumental motivation to learn English is high. Second, as is evident from job advertisements, proficiency in English is a necessary skill for employment in Thailand, particularly in high-paying jobs. In addition, skill in English is important for overseas employment. Both of these factors can contribute to extrinsic instrumental motivation to learn English. Finally, proficiency in English allows Thais to acquire technical and business information not available in the mother tongue; access to this type of information can in the long run produce economic rewards. Many of these same factors are promoting the spread of English in the Philippines, even in the face of strong nationalist sentiments which are seeking to restrict the use of English in favor of the promotion of Pilipino.

The Philippines

The Philippines contrasts with Thailand in that English is a co-official language. Diglossia exists in areas where English is used along with Pilipino on a day-to-day basis, with English being used in many of the domains associated with a High variety and Pilipino in domains associated with a Low variety. According to Pascasio (1988:114), in the Philippines English is used 'mainly in the domains of the school, business, industry, diplomacy, government and the judiciary.' In government, the formal sessions in the Senate and House are conducted in English; in the courts, judges and lawyers conduct their trials in English; in business and industry, English dominates high-level staff meetings; in the mass media, English predominates in the newspapers (ibid.:114-16).

The fact that English is used in these formal domains, domains in which there are many white-collar jobs, suggests that there are several extrinsic sources of instrumental motivation to learn English in the Philippines. Moreover, since Filipinos tend to view English as the key to social mobility and higher paying jobs, intrinsic instrumental motivation is also high. In some ways, English in the Philippines, even more than in Thailand, is viewed as the key to economic mobility. While there are economically successful Thais who do not speak English, there are far fewer economically successful Filipinos who do not speak English. For many Filipinos, economic success is closely associated with the ability to do so. As Pascasio (ibid.:117) says, Filipinos of the lower class identify with 'the values and objectives of the affluent Filipinos who speak English and would like to share this affluence by learning English.'

The results of a survey on the role and status of English in the Philippines by Sibayan (1985), which appears at the end of this chapter, demonstrate how proficiency in English is linked in the minds of many Filipinos to social and economic mobility. As a way of ascertaining why Filipinos are studying English, one of the questions Sibayan asked his 186 key informants, whom he considered to be the élite of the country, was to list what they considered to be the most important reasons for learning English today in the Philippines. The three most cited reasons were: (1) for access to the international community; (2) for social and economic mobility as it relates to getting a good job and a better education, and (3) for better communication among Filipinos in the areas of government, business, academia, and the media (ibid.:23). All these reasons reflect a belief in the instrumental value of English in Filipino life. On the other hand, less instrumental reasons for learning English, such as 'because English is a rich language' or 'because it is part of the Filipino culture,' were ranked very low. As in Thailand, proficiency in English is viewed as closely related to the instrumental goals of gaining access to information, particularly of an international nature, and to social and economic mobility.

Many Filipinos, like Thais, believe that English provides the key to educational, social, and economic advancement. But is this in fact the case? According to Gonzalez, the current economic benefits of speaking English in contemporary Filipino society are quite impressive. As he says:

> certainly in seeking a white-collar job, one cannot be monolingual in Filipino [Pilipino], but one can still be de facto monolingual in English at the upper levels of business; for official communications and at board meetings, English is the predominant language. And in science and technology, even in the provinces, one must switch to English to speak, for example of medical and clinical facts and analyses. At the secondary and tertiary levels of education English still predominates. (Gonzalez 1988b:108)

The ability to speak English is important not only in the domestic job market, but also in the growing international labor market. In 1985 the Philippines Overseas Employment Agency (POEA) sent more than 400,000 workers abroad, mostly to the Middle East. (This total did not include a large number of workers who made arrangements on their own, mostly in domestic, nursing, teaching, and hotel jobs.) A survey of employment agencies accredited by POEA indicates that, for most jobs, a comprehension of spoken English was deemed an absolute necessity (ibid.:110). For Filipinos today, the chances of getting a job, particularly one that pays well, both in the Philippines and abroad, are greatly increased by the ability to speak English.

The ability to speak English also provides an individual with access to important sources of information. A survey done by Sibayan (1985:71-4) on the mass media in the Philippines indicates that almost all of the newspapers and magazines are published in English. Also both of the national news-gathering organizations use English in their dispatches to Manila. Thus, the majority of information on current national and international events and on financial matters is available in English. Another area of information where English predominates is in the field of computers. Currently, all existing computer databases in the Philippines are in English with no plans to transcribe them into Pilipino (ibid.:76).

Proficiency in English in the Philippines is necessary both for gaining access to job possibilities and for obtaining financial news and technical information. Both these facts will undoubtedly contribute to the continued spread of English. The main counter force to this spread is the growing national feeling that Pilipino should be developed as the sole official language so that it can replace English in the domains of government, business, and education.

At the present time, as Gonzalez (1988a:9) points out, the 'linguistic situation in the Philippines creates a dilemma for the Filipinos themselves.' On the one hand, 'the imperatives of nationalism make it an urgent task for Filipino society to develop its national language . . . for symbolic purposes, as a linguistic symbol, of unity and national identity,' as well as for functional purposes, since many young Filipinos are unable to carry on basic communication in English. Today, to show their support for nationalist sentiments, many of the élite are trying to improve their Pilipino. According to Bautista (1988:75) it has come to a point where, particularly in the public fora of Manila, the élite often 'have to apologize for not having fluent control of Filipino, and therefore for resorting to English. The children of the élite are learning Filipino because of its increased presence in the school system and its prevalent availability in the mass media.'

On the other hand, Gonzalez maintains that there are important economic reasons for maintaining English in the Philippines, economic considerations which are perhaps important enough to 'supersede consideration of nationalism.' He argues that

> With nearly two million Filipinos abroad and with the Philippine Overseas Employment Administration (POEA) still sending workers outside the country (nearly half a million yearly) because of population growth and unemployment/underemployment, Filipinos *do* need competence in English for employability. Moreover, for business and international relations, to attract local investments and the transfer of regional offices in other ASEAN [Association of Southeast Asian Nations] countries to Manila more than to Hong Kong or Singapore

. . . skills in English language are needed more than ever. In the long term, more than immediate employability, access to science and technology is possible to Filipinos at present only through English since it will take at least a whole generation if not more to intellectualize Filipino and to make it capable of making knowledge from the West available at an advanced level. (Gonzalez 1988a:9–10)

The question of whether or not economic considerations of nationism will outweigh nationalist sentiments in the Philippines remains to be seen. In the meantime, proficiency in English is popularly viewed, to use Kachru's (1986) term, as an 'alchemy' that can transmute an individual's life.

Conclusion

While the social and political contexts of a country determine the official role of English in society, the economic context can provide incentives for learning English important enough to make individuals desire to learn the language even if it has no official status in society. In many countries, motivation to learn English is high both because individuals regard it as a key to economic mobility and because actual economic rewards exist for knowing it. In countries where English has some official status, like the Philippines and India, it is frequently used in formal domains related to the economic structure of the country. Because of this, individuals often want to know English to be able to operate effectively in the formal domains, domains in which white-collar jobs exist.

The strong association of English with social and economic mobility suggests that many people study it primarily on the basis of instrumental motivation. When students study English for job mobility or to attain specialized information, (1) they may be more interested in learning the vocabulary of business, science, and technology than the vocabulary of literature; (2) they may be more interested in learning to read English in order to gain access to professional information than to speak it, and (3) they will probably be more interested in acquiring formal English than informal English. These three factors are important considerations to keep in mind when designing an English curriculum for such students. As Hutchinson and Waters (1987:6) point out, recent expansion in scientific, technical, and economic activity on an international scale has created 'a whole new mass of people wanting to learn English, not for the pleasure or prestige of knowing the language,' but because English is 'the key to the international currencies of technology and commerce.' Expatriate language teachers need to become aware of the special goals of their students. Why are their students studying English? In what contexts will they be using it? What vocabulary do they need to know? Needs assessment is an important initial step for effective language teaching.

While the political context influences the role and status of English in a country and the economic context affects motivational factors in learning English, another dimension that must be considered in international language teaching is the culture of the country. Classroom roles are culture bound and in cases where students and teachers have different expectations about the classroom, as can occur in expatriate language teaching situations, cultural conflicts may arise. The next chapter examines these potential conflicts.

Exploring the ideas

1 One way in which a society can contribute to the spread of English is by allocating resources to English teaching. As was pointed out on page 31, in reference to Central America, the amount of money that a society devotes to education appears to affect the quality and extent of English teaching. Identify and discuss specific ways in which the amount of available funds can affect the quality and extent of English teaching.

2 This chapter has pointed out several important reasons for the spread of English such as enforced language use through colonialism and a belief in the economic advantages of learning it. What other factors do you think are contributing to the spread of English? In your discussion, consider linguistic features such as the availability of technical vocabulary, as well as social, political, economic, educational, and mass-media factors.

3 The case-study on the Philippines in this chapter refers to the survey done by Sibayan (1985) on the status and role of English *vis-à-vis* Pilipino in the Philippines. In order to determine the relative role and status of the two languages and thus gain insight into the diglossic situation of the Philippines, Sibayan interviewed 186 informants who were leaders in one of four domains—government, business, academia, or the media. The following is the questionnnaire used by Sibayan.

1. In your opinion what is the most important reason for learning English?
2. In your opinion what is the most important reason for learning Pilipino?
3. Do you believe that the propagation of a national language is a necessary condition for the attainment of our national aspirations as a people and a nation?
_____ yes   _____ no

4. In learning English what do you think are the:
a. chief problems?
b. chief inducements?
5. In learning Pilipino what do you think are the:
a. chief problems?
b. chief inducements?
6. When Filipinos who speak different languages meet, what language(s) do they use mostly in the following situations:

Situation	Language Used			
	English	Pilipino	Taglish	Vernacular
day-to-day activities	——	——	——	——
conferences	——	——	——	——
business transactions	——	——	——	——

7. In your opinion do you think the kind of spoken Filipino English that is developing will be:
a. difficult for other Asians to understand
_____ yes   _____ no
b. difficult for native speakers of English to understand?
_____ yes   _____ no
8. Do you think English should be taught only to those who will study in high school and the university?
_____ yes   _____ no
9. Do you think English can be replaced by Pilipino to educate future members of your profession?
_____ yes   _____ no
If yes, how many years will it take? ___
If no, why not?
10. How would you assess the spoken and written English of the following groups today compared with 20 years ago: improved, deteriorated, the same or don't know?

Average elementary school graduate   Average college graduate
    public   Junior executives
    private   Professionals
Average high school graduate   Government employees
    public   Rank and file employees of
    private   private firms

(Sibayan 1985:93-4)

The survey seeks to answer the following questions that were raised in this chapter and Chapter 1. First, why are people choosing to learn English in the Philippines? Are they doing so for integrative or instrumental reasons? How is the use of English in the Philippines related to nationalism and the development of the country's national identity? What inducements exist in the country to learn English? Are they economic? In what domains is English being used in the country? Are these domains related to the economic structure of the country?

If you wanted to investigate these questions in another context, how might you go about answering them, assuming that you were not able to undertake an extensive survey as was done by Sibayan? Discuss the things you might observe in a country and the things you might ask (and who you would ask them to) that would provide some insight into the questions.

4 The following is a description of the role of English in Peru from the British Council English Language Teaching Profile (1982:2). Peru is a country in which English has no official status and is not a required subject of study.

> The role of English in Peru is essentially developmental. English provides the point of contact with the outside world. For business and professional people it is the means of international communication, not only with English speaking countries. On the professional side it is of paramount importance in that all up to date information relating to technological development, medicine, engineering, the sciences, business management, etc. is only available through English. Anyone who wishes to reach a worthwhile level in their field must have at least a reading knowledge.

On the basis of the above description, why might a Peruvian enroll in an English class? Would the individual's motivation most likely be instrumental or integrative? In what domains would the individual be likely to use English—in formal or informal ones? For use within Peru, what skills might be most important to the individual—reading, writing, speaking, or listening? What type of vocabulary instruction might the individual want?

Researching the ideas

1 As was pointed out in the chapter, in countries like Thailand and Tunisia where English has no official status, students may enroll in English classes with very specific goals in mind, whether it be to get a particular job or to be able to read specialized information in English. In order to meet the

particular and specialized needs of their students, expatriate language teachers need to undertake a thorough needs assessment of their class.

In preparation for undertaking your own classroom needs assessment, research the relevant literature. Two references to start with are Nunan's *Learner Centred Curriculum* and Munby's *Communicative Syllabus Design*, listed in the bibliography.

2 As this chapter has demonstrated, in many countries such as Tunisia and Costa Rica, although English has no official status it is spreading because of economic incentives in the scientific and business community. In such countries, because students have very particular reasons for studying English, English for Specific Purposes courses are frequently offered.

In order to prepare yourself for possible involvement in such courses, research the history, assumptions, goals, and current trends of English for Specific Purposes. The following are some sources that will be helpful in this project.

Hutchinson, T. and A. Waters. 1987. *English for Specific Purposes.* Cambridge: Cambridge University Press.

Kennedy, C. and R. Bolitho. 1984. *English for Specific Purposes.* New York: Macmillan.

McDonough, J. 1984. *ESP in Perspective—A Practical Guide.* New York: Collins.

Swales, J. (ed.) 1985. *Episodes in ESP.* Oxford: Pergamon Press.

Widdowson, H.G. 1983. *Learning Purpose and Language Use.* Oxford: Oxford University Press.

The *ESP Journal* is published three times a year by Pergamon Press. Subscriptions are available from the Journal Sales Department, Pergamon Press PLC, Headington Hill Hall, Headington, Oxford, OX3 0BW.

Suggestions for further reading

Brown, H.D. 1987. *Principles of Language Learning and Teaching.* Englewood Cliffs, NJ: Prentice-Hall.
This book provides a good introduction to the relationship between motivation, attitudes, and language learning.

Fishman, J., R. Cooper, and **A. Conrad.** (eds.) 1977. *The Spread of English.* Rowley, Mass.: Newbury House.

A seminal collection of readings on English as a world language, the economic power of English, and attitudes toward its use.

Kachru, B. 1986. *The Alchemy of English.* Oxford: Pergamon Press.
While the majority of the book is devoted to the issue of institutionalized varieties of English, the introduction provides a convincing argument on its linguistic power.

3 LANGUAGE TEACHING AND THE CULTURAL CONTEXT

Theoretical background

Classrooms operate within a cultural context which to a large extent determines not only what is to be learned, but also how it is to be learned. In order to operate effectively within a classroom, students need to be aware of culturally appropriate behavior patterns. As Mehan (1981:48) notes, 'To be competent members of the classroom community, students must not only know what to do, but when and where to do it. Inasmuch as the classroom is a socially organized community, participants must be able to act appropriately within its normative constraints.'

To be competent members of a classroom community, teachers too must know what to do and when and where to do it. Expatriate language teachers may well have very different expectations from their students about what should occur in a classroom community. When teachers and students have different expectations regarding classroom behavior, conflicts can arise. This chapter will focus on cultural differences in classroom expectations and how these differences may create conflict. It will also offer suggestions for dealing with conflict.

To define culture is not an easy task, and while countless definitions exist, most of them include the idea that culture entails socially transmitted patterns regarding both behavior and values. Since in this chapter we are concerned with the relationship between culture and education, it is useful to distinguish the two kinds of education set forth by Heath (1984:1). The first type of education is that which members of a culture acquire from their families, peers, and communities. This type enables individuals 'to learn ways of believing, behaving toward and valuing people' around them. This learning is provided by the culture *outside* the classroom. The second type of education occurs in schools and formal institutions in which knowledge that those in authority wish individuals to learn is transmitted. This learning occurs *inside* the classroom.

What occurs inside a classroom is to some extent a factor of the learning that takes place outside it, but a classroom is a cultural context itself with its own rules of behaving and of valuing people. According to Heath, children educated in their own culture often experience dissonance between what they have learned outside the classroom and what they are expected to learn inside it. This dissonance, however, is likely to be greater in classrooms where the teacher and students, belonging to different cultures, bring different ways of 'believing, behaving toward and valuing people' and different expectations about what should occur inside a classroom.

In this chapter we will examine the relationship between the larger cultural context and the classroom, as well as the classroom itself as a cultural context in which teachers and students behave in particular ways. First, we discuss the classroom itself and point out how expectations regarding the roles of teachers and learners can be affected by the larger cultural context. Next, we discuss some principles of ethnographic research that can be used to obtain a better understanding of cross-cultural differences in classroom expectations. Finally, we consider culture as a topic for learning materials, examining the relationship between language and culture. In the 'Case studies' section we examine two specific teaching situations which demonstrate how cultural differences in classroom expectations can affect the language classroom and how teachers might deal with such differences.

A good deal of research exists to verify the existence of cross-cultural differences in classroom behavior (see, for example, Trueba, Guthrie, and Au 1981, and Trueba 1987); however, most of this research has been undertaken in minority education contexts, i.e. where the students are not part of the mainstream culture. While we are concerned with a different type of classroom, one in which the teacher rather than the student is not a member of the mainstream culture, the findings of microethnographic studies on minority education are valuable in demonstrating the way in which cultural background affects the behavior of teachers and students. We turn now to a summary of several such studies, followed by a discussion of how teachers might approach cultural differences in classroom expectations.

Multicultural classrooms

Multicultural classrooms exist throughout the world, varying tremendously in the composition of the cultural groups involved. In some instances, such classrooms are composed of students from one or more minority ethnic groups while the teacher is from the dominant culture. This is the composition of many of the multicultural classrooms in the United States and Britain. In other instances, however, while most of the students share the same ethnic background, the teacher comes from another culture. This is the situation which expatriate teachers most often encounter. Frequently in a multicultural classroom, teachers and students approach the situation with different expectations about their roles, as well as differing views about the aim of formal education. These different expectations are based both on the teachers' and the students' education outside the classroom, which provided them with different cultural values and behaviors, and on their previous experience within classrooms in different cultures. Often a culture itself supports a particular view of the function of education.

Cultural views about the role of education

In the United States, for example, the concept of competition appears to be at the heart of the formal educational structure (Trueba 1989:37). In schools in the United States, students tend to compete against one another and one of the primary roles of the teacher is to establish who are the winners and who are the losers. As Goldman and McDermott state:

> In a school system that has all children pitted against each other in the name of celebrating the best, we have become preoccupied with documenting and sorting out the half of our children who do not do as well as their fellow citizens. The sorting function of schools is never far away from any classroom. This makes teaching a most difficult task. (Goldman and McDermott 1987:282, as cited in Trueba 1989)

In Japan, in contrast, individual effort rather than competition provides the foundation for education.

> The Japanese believe that hard work, diligence, and perseverance yield success in education as in other aspects of life. . . . The amount of time and effort spent in study are believed to be more important than intelligence in determining educational outcomes. Most Japanese parents and educators are unshakably optimistic that virtually all children have the potential to master the challenging academic curriculum, provided they work hard and long enough. (US Department of Education 1987:3)

The role of the school in Japan then is not to separate stronger students from weaker students, as is done in the United States, but rather to see that all of the students succeed.

Teacher behavior

Since cultures differ in their overall educational goals, it is not surprising that the behavior of teachers also varies cross-culturally. Recent micro-ethnographic studies of minority education suggest that teachers from different cultural backgrounds carry out their roles somewhat differently.

Mohatt and Erickson (1981), for example, investigated differences between a Canadian Indian and a non-Indian teacher, both teaching classes of Odawa Indians in Ontario. They focused on such things as overall tempo of teaching, their overall directiveness of teaching, and the types of structures the teachers used to stimulate speaking in their class-rooms. Based on their analysis of the activities that occurred in both classrooms during eighteen hours of videotaped instruction, Mohatt and Erickson concluded that

> the two teachers relied on strategies based on different participation structures. These strategies reflected different presuppositions about ways of playing out the same kind of scene—cultural presupposi-tions of what is appropriate in ordinary social relations between adults and children. Differences in the teachers' styles of interacting seem to be related to characteristic Odawa Indian participation structures, in contrast to non-Indian ones. (Mohatt and Erickson 1981:117)

During the taped lessons, the two teachers exhibited different types of behavior based on the patterns of adult-child relationships promoted in their subculture. For example, while the non-Indian teacher frequently designated periods of free time as opposed to work time, the Indian teacher did not overtly make such a distinction. Mohatt and Erickson contend that this was because the Indian teacher was adhering to a model of participation in keeping with Indian traditions where 'leadership by teacher and student interpenetrate and is not divided into separate compartments' (ibid.:112). They maintain that the teacher clearly had control of the students, but achieved this by paying attention to the rhythms of student activity and judging when the students were ready for activities to change. Their findings illustrate how the cultural values that a teacher acquires outside the classroom can affect his or her classroom behavior.

Student behavior

Cross-cultural differences also play a part in students' behavior. One way students take an active role in a classroom is by asking and answering questions. Sato (1982) studied the classroom participation patterns of Asian (Chinese, Japanese, and Korean) and non-Asian (Latin American, European, and Middle Eastern) students in two university ESL courses. She found that Asian students took significantly fewer speaking turns than their non-Asian classmates and were called upon less often by the teacher. Although Asian students comprised almost 61 per cent of the class, they took only 37 per cent of the turns. Furthermore, the behavior of the Asian students in seeking out opportunities to speak suggested that they felt a stronger need than did non-Asian students to get a 'go ahead' from the teacher before speaking in the class. Sato's study, as she notes, provides 'some preliminary evidence for the role of ethnic styles in classroom discourse' (ibid. 21).

Implications for language teaching

The studies cited above demonstrate that both teachers' and students' classroom behavior are affected by their cultural background. It is therefore quite likely that you and your students will have different views concerning your roles and what should occur in a classroom. What approach can you take to deal with these differences? First, it is important for you to gain an understanding of your students' expectations regarding classroom behavior. Shortly we will examine how the principles of ethnographic research might be used to investigate students' expectations. Second, you should take measures to clarify your own views as to the appropriate role of teachers and students. These views will inevitably have been influenced by your own culture for, as Spindler (1974:153) says, in reference to teachers, 'they are *products of their culture* and live within the framework of values and symbols that are part of that culture.' While an inquiry into cross-cultural differences in classroom expectations is extremely important, it is unrealistic to think that either you or your students can modify your behavior so that there is total congruence in your expectations.

A more realistic approach may be for you to negotiate with your students (and if necessary with their administrator) for ways to accommodate the cultural differences that exist. Such an approach was undertaken by Harvey (1985) in his teaching post at Tianjin University, one of China's most prestigious science and technology institutions. Harvey found that among his students

> there was a considerable amount of careful, painstaking translation of text; a tendency to memorize dialogues, whether this was required or not; a great interest in grammatical analysis; a strong desire to be corrected whenever a mistake occurred; and the prospect of even informal 'tests' threw everyone into a panic. (Harvey 1985:185)

The behavior of Harvey's students reflects a Chinese perspective of learning: 'Even now the most widely accepted view of learning in China is that it is memory-based. The teacher or textbook has the knowledge. In order to acquire it, it is sufficient for the students to commit it to memory' (Maley 1986:104).

Although the students in Harvey's class showed a strong preference for memory-based learning activities, he found that they were willing to participate in teaching activities with which they were not familiar if the rationale was explained. Given the fact that the students were open to change if reasons were explained, he involved them in several discussions on the differences between western and Chinese study methods. He and the students then attempted to label each of the western techniques as 'constructive' or 'non-constructive' in terms of the goals the students wanted to achieve at the end of the course.

The stance taken by Harvey may be a workable one for many situations. It is not reasonable to expect that students will want or be able to accept all types of language teaching methods. As Maley (1986:109) points out, 'it is a mistake for the foreign teacher to arrive thinking he has brought the good news in the form of up-to-date methods and materials.' On the other hand, you will have certain beliefs as to what methodologies are preferable and certain assumptions about the role of a teacher and student in a classroom, and these should not be abandoned too easily.

What Harvey is suggesting is that in contexts where the students and teacher share different learning assumptions, they need to discuss these differences and negotiate a curriculum based on the needs and skills of the students. In this way specific classroom techniques are not labeled as 'good' or 'bad' but as effective or ineffective in terms of helping students to reach their goals in learning English. If you find yourself in a situation where the administration or students, or possibly both, are unable or unwilling to negotiate a curriculum, and you find it difficult to accept this assumption about language teaching, then you will need to seriously consider whether or not you want to retain your post. In order to provide strategies for dealing with cultural differences, we turn now to a discussion of ethnographic principles and suggest how some of these might be applied.

Ethnography

Principles of ethnography

Originally ethnographic research was related to the study of what were called 'primitive societies' (Damen 1987:57). Today, however, the meaning of the term 'ethnography' has been broadened and it can be defined more appropriately as 'the study of the world of a people' (Yates 1986:61). Its goal is to describe and interpret how people interact in a setting such as a classroom, neighborhood, or community and to explain the meaning these interactions have for the participants (Watson-Gegeo 1988:576).

One of the central principles of ethnographic research, as it is currently conceived, is that cultures should be studied from the viewpoint of members of the culture. Such a perspective has been termed *emic*. This term, along with its counterpart *etic*, which refers to the study of cultures from an external perspective, are abbreviated forms of Kenneth Pike's distinction between a phon*emic* and phon*etic* analysis of sound systems. While a phonetic analysis seeks to universally describe all human sounds, a phonemic analysis describes sound distinctions that are relevant to a particular language. This distinction was further extended by Pike to human behavior in general:

> In contrast to the *Etic* approach, an *Emic* one is in essence valid for only one language (or one culture) at a time. . . . An *etic* analytical standpoint . . . might be called 'external' or 'alien', since for *etic* purposes the analyst stands 'far enough away' from or 'outside' of a particular culture to see its separate events, primarily in relation to their similarities and their differences, as compared to the events of other cultures. (Pike 1954:8–10)

The advantage of studying a culture from an emic perspective is that such an approach may minimize a tendency to be ethnocentric. In fact, a primary goal of ethnographic research is to understand a culture in its own right. As Damen states, the goals of ethnographic research are based on the tenet

> that any efforts aimed at understanding another culture should be guided toward the identification of salient cultural patterns and themes, that all efforts should be made to overcome ethnocentric bondage and blindness, that the internal 'logic' of given cultural systems provides a unique 'world view' for their bearers, that this world view is best conveyed by reference to the perceptions of those who share these patterns, and that no cultural group should be judged as being inherently superior or inferior to another. (Damen 1987:58)

By advocating that researchers adopt an emic perspective, ethnographic research strives to free researchers from imposing their own cultural biases on another culture.

Ethnographic research has two additional principles that are relevant to our discussion. First, such research focuses on behavior within a group; hence, if an ethnographer is studying a language classroom, the focus would be on the class as a group of learners operating within a particular social setting rather than on any individual learner. Second, 'ethnography is holistic; that is, any aspect of a culture or behavior has to be described and explained in relation to the whole system of which it is a part' (Watson-Gegeo 1988:577). Because of this, a particular interaction in a classroom would be considered within the larger framework of the classroom, the school, the school administration, and the society in general.

Implications for language teaching

In order to gain a better understanding of cross-cultural differences in the classroom, expatriate language teachers can draw on the principles of ethnography. Like ethnographers, teachers can examine the behavior of their students holistically, trying to understand how their classroom behavior is influenced by larger cultural issues like religious beliefs or the role of women in society. By examining the relationship between their students' learning outside the classroom and their behavior in the classroom, teachers will gain a better understanding of why their students act as they do. In addition, like ethnographers, teachers can try to understand the classroom community within which they are operating in its own right and to put aside their own cultural assumptions about what should or should not occur in a classroom. In this way they can work to attain an emic perspective.

One way in which an emic perspective can be developed is to undertake limited ethnographic research projects, or what Damen (1987:63) terms *pragmatic ethnography*. She outlines a procedure which can be applied to specific overseas teaching contexts (ibid.:64–9).

Pragmatic ethnography

1 Choosing a target group Choose a target group that you would like to investigate. You could select the culture in which you are teaching or would like to teach.

2 Choosing informants Select informants who are native to the culture and can therefore provide an emic perspective.

3 Providing a foundation for inquiry Provide a foundation for your inquiry by investigating secondary sources about classroom behavior in the culture.

4 Informant interviewing Undertake extensive interviews (at least four or five hour-long interviews) with your informants about classroom behavior in the target group you are investigating. Decide in advance the questions you want to ask and seek permission to take notes or record the interview. Damen suggests that the researcher start with descriptive questions such as the following: 'Can you give me an example of a disruptive or troublesome student? What would such a student do?' (Question number two in the 'Researching the ideas' section at the end of this chapter includes some sample interview questions.)

5 Analyzing data and forming cultural hypotheses Analyze the information gathered from your secondary sources and from the interviews to arrive at some hypotheses about the expected classroom behavior patterns of the culture.

6 Looking in the mirror Stop to determine your own values regarding the roles of teachers and students and try to determine how representative they are of your own culture.

7 Putting theory and knowledge to work Try to apply the understanding you gained from your inquiry into the culture to your development of materials, lesson plans, and classroom management.

This model provides teachers with a practical method for trying to understand and cope with cross-cultural differences in the classroom. It has three essential stages: *inquiry* (steps 1 to 4) in which teachers gather information on a particular culture through reading and extensive interviews; *reflection* (steps 5 to 6) in which teachers form generalizations regarding another culture based on their inquiry and consider their own values on a particular topic, and *application* (step 7) in which teachers apply their knowledge to their particular classroom situation. In many ways, the third stage is the most difficult for it necessitates teachers devising ways to accommodate the differences which exist between their own and their learners' expectations. This process of accommodation will typically require changes on the part of both the teacher and the learner, changes which may be difficult for both. In the 'Case studies' section we will examine several situations which required difficult adjustments on the part of expatriate language teachers and their students.

In addition to affecting the role of teachers and learners in the classroom, cultural issues also affect the selection of teaching materials. Because language provides a vehicle for transmitting a culture and to some extent channels the way its members perceive the world, it has been argued that in order to learn a second language, one must learn the culture. As Brown (1987:33) puts it, 'second language learning is often second culture learning.' Educators who support this position advocate using English-teaching materials which contain a good deal of cultural information about anglophone countries. Others, however, argue that English, as a growing international language, does not belong to any one particular culture and as such should be taught using cultural information which relates to the local culture. This view is particularly strong in Uni-modal countries like Malaysia where the teaching of another culture is viewed as a deterrent to the building of nationalism. We turn now to the issue of cultural content in English teaching materials.

Culture in materials

Dimensions of culture

Adaskou, Britten, and Fahsi (1989) point out that language teaching may involve various dimensions of culture. First, there is the *aesthetic sense* in which a language is associated with the literature, film, and music of a particular country. Language teaching materials may, for example, be based on literary texts. Next, there is the *sociological sense* of a culture in which a language is linked to the customs and institutions of a country. If a curriculum promotes the sociological sense of culture, the materials include information about such things as family life, education, and holidays.

Third, there is the *semantic sense* in which a culture's conceptual system is embodied in the language. This, in turn, conditions the culture's perceptions and thought processes. In order to teach this semantic sense of a culture, classroom materials might include, for example, the vocabulary needed to describe family relationships, vocabulary for which there might be no direct equivalents in the learner's mother tongue. Finally, there is the *pragmatic sense* of a culture which determines what language is appropriate for what contexts. If the curriculum deals with this sense of culture, classroom materials might include such items as how to politely refuse an invitation or how to complain about services. To the extent that such rules of speaking differ cross-culturally, it is difficult to know whose culturally determined standards of politeness to apply in a curriculum. This is an issue that we will examine in the next chapter under the question of standards.

Adaskou, Britten, and Fahsi (ibid.:3) maintain that the last two senses of culture—the pragmatic and to a lesser degree the semantic—are necessary to the development of communicative competence since, in order to be competent in a language, individuals need to understand the concepts that individual words embody as well as how to use the words appropriately. Thus, to be fluent in English a speaker needs to know the semantic distinction between such words as a 'feast' and a 'meal' or an 'accident' and a 'catastrophe'. In addition, they need to understand the pragmatic force of a phrase, knowing, for example, when 'It's cold' is a statement and when it is a request. On the other hand, Adaskou, Britten, and Fahsi suggest that the main arguments for including material relating to the aesthetic and sociological dimensions of culture in a curriculum involve such goals as fostering international understanding, motivating learners, and facilitating the learners' possible future visits to foreign countries.

In some circumstances it might be argued that there are sound pedagogical reasons for including all four dimensions of culture in the curriculum, but in other instances local leaders do not want to encourage the teaching of another culture or even to use any cultural content at all. Alptekin and Alptekin, for example, point out that in China and Korea the pedagogical focus seems to be on the grammatical features of English with little attention to cultural content; furthermore, they argue, in many places in Asia and parts of Africa and Latin America, there is a feeling on the part of the educated élite that English instruction in particular and modernization in general which has not been 'acculturated' and shaped to fit the country's needs constitutes a threat to national identity. Because of this, suggestions have been made to 'de-Anglo-Americanize' English, both in linguistic and cultural aspects. (Alptekin and Alptekin 1984:14–15)

The idea of 'de-Anglo-Americanizing' the English curriculum is strongly advocated by Ndebele in reference to South Africa; he maintains that

> what may need to be emphasized is that if the recognition that English belongs to all who use it is more than academic, then in multi-cultural societies, English will have to be taught in such a way that the learners are made to recognize themselves through the learning content employed, not as second class learners of a foreign culture, or as units of labour that have to be tuned to work better, but as self-respecting citizens of the world. The idea of teaching English through the exposure of second language learners to English culture should be abandoned. If English belongs to all, then it will naturally assume the cultural colour of its respective users. (Ndebele 1986:13–14)

In the 1980s, when Morocco was involved in a large-scale textbook development project for secondary schools, the steering committee interviewed and questioned teachers, inspectors, and teacher trainers in order to determine to what extent they believed the textbooks should include a cultural component which related to an anglophone country. The following are three questions on cultural content asked of the informants, along with the responses of the teachers. (Note that the biased nature of the questions may have affected the responses.)

> 1. Can the use of a foreign milieu, by inviting cultural comparisons, contribute to students' discontent with their own material culture and to the yearning for the big city and the fleshpots of Europe?
> *Most English teachers feel that it can.*
>
> 2. Are there patterns of behaviour in an English-speaking social context that most Moroccans would prefer not to see presented as models to their young people?
> *Again, the commonest answer is yes.*
>
> 3. Will Moroccan secondary learners still be motivated to learn English if the language is not presented to them, as it has been up to now, in the context of an English-speaking country?
> *Here the consensus . . . is that today's secondary learners are not less but more motivated to learn English when it is presented in contexts that relate its use realistically to their lives as young adults in Morocco.*
> (Adaskou, Britten, and Fahsi 1989:7)

On the basis of the results of this survey, the textbook committee decided that over ninety per cent of the regional content of the coursebooks would be situated in Morocco with more than half of the characters Moroccan. In addition, all of the Anglo-American cultural content would be restricted to the pragmatic and semantic senses of culture referred to above (ibid.:1989:8).

Another country which has elected to use local topics and literature in their curriculum is the Philippines. Sibayan (1985:51) points out that when instructional materials for English were first imported from the United States to the Philippines, problems arose because many of the topics used were unsuitable for Filipino children. Thus, the children had no idea what was meant by 'snow', 'apples', 'winter', and 'spring'. As it became obvious that such materials were inappropriate for use in the Philippines, the Bureau of Education began to develop its own series of books, containing prose and poetry by Filipino writers who used English to picture Filipino life and culture.

Implications for language teaching

The fact that such controversy surrounds the use of cultural materials in the classroom suggests that expatriate language teachers need to be aware of the cultural content that is in a text. Even very basic language teaching materials may entail some cultural information, as is illustrated by the following questions which appear in a language textbook by Boyd and Boyd.

> Do we keep meat in a refrigerator?
> [In developing countries, many people may not have refrigerators; vegetarian cultures may find this sentence offensive.]
>
> Do we keep shoes and boots in a closet?
> [In Japan people would never bring shoes into the house.]
>
> Do we keep a bird in a cage?
> [The idea of having birds as pets may be foreign to some cultures.]
> (Boyd and Boyd 1986:47)

These examples demonstrate how even simple statements in a text contain cultural information. Both what Adaskou, Britten, and Fahsi (1989) call 'the semantic sense of culture' and 'the sociological sense of culture' are relevant to the sentences above. Students need not only to understand how shoes and boots differ (a semantic factor), but also where shoes and boots are kept in certain cultures (a sociological factor).

Determining the amount of cultural information presented in a text, or what Damen (1987:259) calls its 'cultural load', entails a detached assessment of the material, a true emic perspective. As Damen says, weighing the cultural load calls for pushing aside the natural cultural screen and assessing the cultural content with as much detachment as we do the linguistic content of a textbook. We must, in fact, step outside our own cultural identities and walk in the shoes of others if we are to make honest evaluations and suitable selections. (Damen 1987:259)

There are several things that can help in assessing the cultural load of a text. First, you could engage in the stages of inquiry described on pages 54–5, thus gaining the background knowledge needed to interpret a text from an emic perspective. For example, in reading about Japanese culture, you would be likely to come across the information that Japanese people rarely bring their shoes into the house. This stage of inquiry can also involve discussing texts with local teachers, asking them to pinpoint culturally difficult passages. You could return the favor by explaining the significance of cultural references, should the local teacher request this.

Second, you could can use your students' interpretation of a text to help them discover what aspects are culturally difficult. If, for example, a Japanese student responded 'No' to the question 'Do we keep shoes and boots in a closet?' by questioning the reasoning behind the student's response and asking where such things are kept, you could gain an understanding of what led the student to respond in this way.

Finally, in terms of assessing the cultural load of a text on a semantic level, knowledge of the local language is essential. For example, while in English there is a separate word for 'finger' and 'toe', in Spanish there is only one word, '*dedo*'. This could lead a Spanish speaker to initially assume that the words 'finger' and 'toe', are synonyms in English. Being familiar with the native language will help in the prediction of such semantic interference.

In addition to being aware of the cultural content of teaching materials, expatriate language teachers need to recognize that ultimately it is local educators who should determine this. When, as a guest, you are asked to teach aspects of your own culture, then by all means you should do so. However, the learning of another culture should never be a one-way street; it is equally important to learn about the culture in which you are living. As Alptekin and Alptekin point out,

> the conflict between the opposing pedagogical views of the 'hosts' and the 'guest' teachers of EFL is in many cases exacerbated by the latter's ignorance of the ways and minds of the local people and their language. In fact, it is quite ironic that, while espousing the idea that foreign language acquisition is a means to increase cross-cultural awareness and sensitivity, the guest teachers are often unable to understand the host culture or to speak the local vernacular. Another

irony lies in their attempts to expose their students to the norms and values of the English-speaking culture in the students' own setting, while very often they themselves continue to remain monolingual and monocultural there. (Alptekin and Alptekin 1984:16)

Expatriate language teachers, as has been pointed out throughout the chapter, need to learn as much as possible about their host culture.

In order to illustrate the manner in which culture can affect the classroom in terms of such things as materials selection and student behavior, we turn now to two case studies of expatriate teachers. The cases are from two non-western countries, Saudi Arabia and Japan. In both cases, the teachers are confronted with teaching problems in their classroom— caused by cross-cultural differences—which they deal with in a particular way. The inclusion of these case studies is not meant to suggest that the way these teachers address their problems is the best or only way the problem could be handled. In fact, in the 'Exploring ideas' section of the chapter, you are asked to reflect on other possible ways of approaching these particular conflicts.

As was pointed out earlier in the chapter, one principle of ethnography that is applicable to language teaching overseas is the emphasis on viewing behavior from a larger perspective, recognizing that specific classroom behavior is influenced by the social, political, economic, and cultural contexts of a society. In the case study which follows, the teacher explains how the cultural values of the society in which she was working, in partic- ular regarding religion and personal relationships, influenced her teaching. The study illustrates how teachers and students can have very different expectations about what should occur in a classroom. In this case, the teacher, an American, held to a widely accepted American value that education and religion should be separated. In addition, she believed that school commitments should take priority over personal commitments. These views, however, were not shared by her students. The lack of a match between the teacher's and students' expectations resulted in the teacher modifying her selection of classroom materials and her homework assignments.

Case studies

Saudi Arabia

In 1980 Constance Joy, an American, joined a group of expatriate English teachers working in Saudi Arabia. For five and a half years, from 1980 to 1985, she taught English at Al Nahda Women's Philanthropic Society, a women's school in Riyadh. The private school where Joy worked was established in 1962 by Princess Sarah, the daughter of King Faisal, as a setting where women could do charitable work and study such things as French, English, sewing, and typing. The program had an enrolment of approximately 400 students, mostly housewives, from the age of 16 through 50. The staff of 15 teachers were expatriates, many of whom were the wives of British Council employees.

In 1985 Joy examined her teaching experience in a master's thesis in which she presented guidelines for prospective English teachers in Saudi Arabia. The following is a partial summary of her work, highlighting the manner in which she perceived cultural factors to be operative in her teaching experience. According to Joy, both religious values and cultural assumptions about personal relationships had a significant effect on her teaching.

Religion

While in the United States every effort is made to separate religion and education, in Saudi Arabia religion dominates every aspect of life. Both the government and the schools view their primary role as promoting religious values. According to Joy (1985), religious factors affected her classroom in the very practical concern of materials selection. Since, according to the tenets of Wahabi Islam, women are not to socialize with men other than family members, education is sexually segregated. Because of this fact, the language curriculum has to cater specifically to the interests of each sex. Women study topics dealing with household tasks such as cooking or sewing. Other topics, however, such as checking accounts and travel arrangements, while common concerns for women in some cultures, are generally undertaken by the men in Saudi Arabia and are not considered appropriate topics for an English course for women. This illustrates the fact that expatriate language teachers cannot assume that what are appropriate classroom topics in one culture will be equally appropriate in another. Instead, they need to try to gain an emic perspective of the culture in which they are working and to carefully assess all language materials in light of the cultural milieu in which they are being used.

Since, according to Islamic tradition, most marriages in Saudi Arabia are arranged and the drinking of alcohol is forbidden, materials which deal with dating or western-style parties are not appropriate for use. In fact, as Joy points out,

> teachers are asked to go through their materials with black magic markers and cover bare midriffs, cleavages, churches, crosses and religious pictures as well as words like beer and wine. . . . Perhaps

the most startling aspect of this censorship to Westerners is that some very religious Wahabis believe that music is immoral, so that any listening material containing music may be condemned by individual students. (Joy 1985:11)

This suggests that expatriate language teachers teaching Wahabis need to select materials without music or risk the chance of alienating their students. The fact that the use of music is considered by some to be immoral is the kind of useful knowledge teachers will gain if they engage in the pragmatic ethnography described earlier in the chapter. Joy also found that many students were quite interested in learning religious vocabulary in English so that they could explain such things as pilgrimages and fasting to foreigners. Religious factors then were of paramount importance in determining what constituted appropriate classroom materials and what would interest the students.

Religious factors can also influence how students in Saudi Arabia approach a reading text. According to Osterloh (1986:78), 'in Islamic countries, the Koran is in the back of the reader's mind when dealing with a text. Hence, what is written is necessarily associated with absolute truth.' Because of this fact, Osterloh contends that in order for a student in an Islamic country to analyze a text and test its validity, he 'will have to go through a series of new social experiences. He has to learn that in Western civilization something written is something man-made, and that everything is to be seen as an individual presentation or personal opinion that can be contested' (ibid.). Osterloh further maintains that students in Islamic countries tend to regard a text 'as a fixed unit in which everything is of equal importance' (ibid.). Hence, such students have difficulty in distinguishing between important and unimportant information. Religion then affects not only what is appropriate reading material in Saudi Arabia, but also how it is approached.

What this suggests for expatriate language teachers is that a reading task which asks Saudi Arabian students to criticize or prioritize parts of a text would be difficult for the students. Furthermore, teachers working with such students would need to consider to what extent this skill was needed. Unless students were going to study in a western environment, such an approach to reading might not be necessary. Making a decision not to emphasize critical reading depends on teachers investigating the culture in which they are teaching so that they are aware of the role of texts in the culture, and then making a decision, based on the needs of the students.

Personal relationships

Another cultural factor which affected Joy's teaching in Saudi Arabia was the area of personal relationships. 'Personal relationships are extremely important to Middle Easterners. For them, the central thing in life is people—family and friendships' (Parker *et al.* 1986:97). Joy, in her experience in Saudi Arabia, found that a great deal of daily life is run on the basis of having a connection with someone in power: 'Getting something done, even for teachers, may mean knowing someone, or being able to use a name effectively' (Joy 1985:16). Family connections can even affect such things as grading since a low grade given to an individual of high status can have a negative effect on the school. As Joy (ibid.:17–18) notes, 'Occasionally, princes and persons of high status complain to administrators with the result that a teacher is fired unfairly, a small class doomed to be shut is kept open . . . a class is cancelled or extended.' When teaching in a cultural context like Saudi Arabia where decisions are based on personal relationships, an expatriate language teacher would need to try to understand why personal relationships have such weight in the culture. He or she would need to work towards attaining an emic perspective, and then to consider to what extent he or she was willing to alter their behavior to deal with the importance of personal relationships.

The importance of developing personal relationships also affected the amount of homework Joy could assign. She found that students devoted a good deal of time to visiting friends and relatives in the evening, a commitment which they considered far more important than doing homework. Because of this, Joy decided to limit her outside assignments, a decision which reflects a willingness on her part to modify her expectations on homework to deal with her students' commitment to their friends. This valuing of personal relationships among Joy's students is in keeping with the generalization made by Parker *et al.* (1986:98) regarding Middle Eastern friendships: 'To his two or three friends, the Middle Easterner will give generously of himself and his time. On each side there will be a sense of affection, of closeness, and of mutual obligation in time of need.'

Joy found that personal relationships could also result in hostility between students in a class. Students who come from warring tribes of the past might not even speak to each other. She found that one solution to this situation was 'to be sensitive to hostilities resulting from family background . . . and not to insist upon group or pair work by students who were absolutely adamant in their dislike for one another' (1985:19). Joy's experience illustrates how values related to religion and personal relationships, values acquired outside of the classroom, can affect what occurs in a classroom in the very practical concerns of materials selection, student grouping, and homework assignments. Thus, to be effective as a language teacher, Joy needed to become sensitive to factors relating to the larger social and cultural context in making classroom decisions. As Osterloh notes, to be able to communicate in the Arab World, Westerners must go through new social experiences—ones they have not encountered in their own culture. Above all they have to reactivate certain of their perceptive and communicative faculties, thus taking them far beyond the goal of mere linguistic language training. (Osterloh 1986:84)

Japan

The need to go beyond mere linguistic training and to become sensitive to the larger social and cultural context was also true for Linda Veno-Kan in her teaching experience in Japan, an experience which illustrates how pragmatic ethnography can be applied to overseas teaching. Pragmatic ethnography, as mentioned earlier, has three essential steps: first, *inquiry*, i.e. studying the assumptions about classroom behavior that are prevalent in the culture through extensive interviews and reading; second, *reflection*, i.e. considering one's own values regarding classroom behavior, and third, *application*, i.e. using one's findings to develop appropriate materials and lesson plans and to manage classroom behavior. Veno-Kan applied this overall strategy to her teaching experience in Japan. As you read the account, consider what other decisions Veno-Kan could have made in trying to accommodate the differences that she and her students had, decisions that might have necessitated more change on her part and less change on the part of the students.

In 1984 Linda Veno-Kan began teaching English at Tokyo Foreign Language College; in 1987 she wrote about her teaching experience in her master's thesis for the School of International Training at Brattleboro, Vermont (Veno-Kan 1987). The following is a partial summary of her thesis.

Tokyo Foreign Language College is a two-year technical college for students who fail their university entrance examination and therefore want to learn English as a way of enhancing their employment possibilities. Because of this, most of the students have high instrumental motivation to learn English. Students are in class five hours per day, five days a week in classes of from twenty-six to fifty students. The majority of the students are females who just graduated from high school.

Although Veno-Kan worked in Japan for over three years and was married to a Japanese, she found that she encountered many cultural misunderstandings in her role as an English teacher. In coping with these misunderstandings, she maintains that she typically adhered to the following procedure in trying to resolve her classroom difficulties.

To begin, she would pinpoint what it was about the students' behavior that seemed to be causing her problems. For example, she found that one frustration she had in class was that her students often responded with silence when she asked them a question. Next, she discussed the difficulties she was having with Japanese friends and did some reading on the topic, undertaking some preliminary inquiry into the area of cultural difference that was causing difficulty. In the case of her students' silence, Veno-Kan learned from her reading that silence in Japan is considered the best response when someone is not certain of the correct reply to a question.

The next thing she did was to reflect on what would be the typical classroom behavior pattern of American students. For example, again in relation to her students' silence, she concluded that in the United States, when a teacher asks a question, students are expected to answer the question or to respond with something like 'I don't know' or 'I don't understand.' In this way Veno-Kan tried to clarify her own culturally determined views on classroom participation.

She then examined how these different classroom expectations affected her teaching. In this case, she found that the students' silence frustrated her, impeding open classroom discussions. Finally, she decided on a strategy to alter the classroom behavior of both herself and her students so that they could accommodate their differences. In the case of the students' silence and their general hesitancy about responding in class, Veno-Kan decided to try to encourage student participation by putting them in groups of four since she believed this would be less intimating for the students than speaking in front of the whole class. She prefaced the group work, however, by explaining to the students her rationale for doing this, telling them that they needed to speak English to learn it. Like Harvey and his experience in China, she found that her students were much more willing to experiment with activities they were not used to if they were given a rationale for doing so.

Throughout her teaching experience in Japan, Veno-Kan tried to apply this procedure to her classroom situation. She consistently tried to pinpoint what was causing cultural misunderstandings between herself and her students, investigate Japanese cultural assumptions, reflect on her own assumptions, and then design classroom activities that would accommodate these differences, a procedure which adheres to the three stages of pragmatic ethnography.

The roles of teachers and students

A good deal of the cultural misunderstanding that occurred in Veno-Kan's class was the result of that fact that she and her students held different expectations about the proper roles of teachers and students. Veno-Kan, as an American teacher, saw her main responsibility to her students as one related to the content of the class rather than to her students' personal concerns. In addition, like Joy, she assumed that students should regard class tasks as more important than personal commitments. Finally, she viewed attendance as an important student responsibility. In her case, as in Joy's, her assumptions were not shared by her students.

In her role as *sensei* (teacher) in Japan, Veno-Kan found that she was not only expected to teach but also to be a parent figure or counselor, to give advice on all kinds of things. Her experience supports the following generalization regarding teachers' roles in Japan:

> Japanese society entrusts major responsibilities to teachers and expects much from them. It confers high social status and economic rewards but also subjects teachers to constant public scrutiny. . . . Teachers are expected to infuse cultural values throughout school activities and to be concerned about students' lives both in and out of school. Their efforts and influence often extend into the home and the community. (US Department of Education 1987:15).

In keeping with this view of the role of a teacher, Veno-Kan's students came to her office for advice on just about anything—'ESL study programs abroad, writing letters to penpals, grades, personal feelings about teachers, financial difficulties, or problems with other students' (1987:22). Giving such advice consumed a lot of time and made Veno-Kan feel uncomfortable. In order to discourage students from seeking this type of advice, particularly in their journal entries written for the teacher, Veno-Kan decided to give her students designated writing topics. She also talked with them about the fact that while American teachers are quite happy to help with class-related questions, they generally do not give personal advice; rather students go to a college counselor. Both these solutions represent little accommodation on Veno-Kan's part since her students, based on what they had learned outside the classroom about the role of a teacher, expected teachers to be sensitive to personal needs. The fact that Veno-Kan did not directly deal with this need reflects a lack of emic perspective on her part, a failure which likely caused her students great frustration.

Not only did Veno-Kan and her students have different expectations regarding the role of a teacher, they also placed different values on the students' relationship with one another. Veno-Kan found she was frustrated by the fact that whenever she assigned group work, her students seemed more concerned with their relationship with one another than with the task at hand (ibid.:48-53). Upon reflecting on her frustration, she concluded that she and her students had different views on the role of an individual in a group. As she says, among Japanese, 'obligations and expectations among the members of the group are exacting; members of a group know each other exceedingly well—one's family life, love affairs, even the limits of one's capacity for cocktails are intimately known to the others' (Nakane, as cited in Veno-Kan, ibid.:51).

From Veno-Kan's perspective, however, the students' interest in one another within the group impeded their ability to complete a given group task. In order to deal with these different classroom expectations, she decided to do several things. First, she asked that group tasks be completed within a specified time period and gave extra points to groups that completed them on time. She also changed round members of groups so that the same people were not always together. Veno-Kan's problem with group work made her aware of the value she placed on getting down to the job at hand and not wasting time. Her own cultural expectations made her feel that her students were not taking the class seriously; yet upon reflection, she decided that this was not necessarily the right inter-pretation: it was rather that students were valuing their relationship with one another more than the task, a conclusion which in this case reflects an effort on her part to attain an emic perspective of her students' behavior.

Another way in which Veno-Kan's classroom expectations did not match those of her students was in the area of absences and tardiness (ibid.:59-63). Many of her students would regularly come to class twenty to thirty minutes late without an excuse; others would show up only on the day of a test or the day a project was due. In discussing this fact with her colleagues, Veno-Kan learned that many Japanese universities and colleges do not keep a record of attendance; rather the school, in admitting students, implies that they are capable of doing the work and thus they need only take the exams and pass them. If students believe they can do this without attending classes, then they may do so. Such assumptions regarding attendance were quite different from her own. In order to deal with these differences, Veno-Kan decided to explain to her students the value she placed on attendance and punctuality; she also established a policy for lateness and absences whereby both poor attendance and consistent tardiness affected the students' final grades. This decision again represents little accommodation on her part which may have resulted in a good deal of frustration for her students.

There were many cultural differences that affected Veno-Kan's teaching experience in Japan. In each case, however, Veno-Kan tried to understand the behavior of her students, to clarify her own values, and to plan class activities that would minimize the differences, decisions that in some instances might have involved more accommodation on her part. However, as she says, by examining the misunderstandings that occurred in her class, she learned a great deal about herself, and she began to reflect upon her teaching much more carefully (ibid.:66).

Conclusion

Both case studies demonstrate how teaching English internationally requires teachers to carefully examine their own assumptions about their role. Expatriate language teachers must, as Osterloh (1986:84) points out, 'go through new social experiences—ones they have not encountered in their own culture.' While undergoing this process teachers should strive to gain an emic perspective of the culture, attempting to view it in its own right and making every effort to overcome enthnocentrism. To attain this emic perspective, they need to view the classroom behavior of their students holistically, as part of a larger cultural framework.

In making decisions about what approach to take to cross-cultural misunderstandings in the classroom, teachers can draw on the model of pragmatic ethnography, employing the three stages of inquiry, reflection, and application. The stage of inquiry, of reading and discussing cultural differences with people of the host country, is essential to understanding why it is that students act as they do. And in dealing with cultural differences, it is important for teachers to realize that they must, to some degree, accommodate to their students' expectations and needs.

Teachers also need to modify their expectations about what is to be learned and how it is to be learned. In terms of selecting classroom materials, expatriate language teachers need to carefully assess the cultural load of the materials they are using and be sensitive to the wishes of local educators regarding whether or not to use materials based on anglophone cultures.

Up to this point we have focused on how contexts outside of the school system itself—the political, economic, and cultural—affect what occurs in a classroom. We turn now to investigating how the educational context of a country, as well as the context of the individual educational institution, can affect overseas teaching. Both contexts place certain constraints on what can occur in a classroom through such things as curriculum guidelines, classroom management policies, and material resources. All of these will directly affect the expatriate language teacher.

Exploring the ideas

1 Adaskou, Britten, and Fahsi (1989) describe four dimensions of culture that can exist in language teaching materials: aesthetic, sociological, semantic, and pragmatic. As was pointed out in the chapter, expatriate language teachers need to be aware of what cultural information exists in a text so that they can assess its cultural load.

   In order to gain experience in this process, assess the cultural load, in the sociological and semantic senses described on page 56, of the passage below.

To assess the cultural load in the sociological sense, list the areas that might cause problems for a reader from a different culture.

Example:
– the appropriate time to arrive at a party
– the roles of host and hostess in preparing for a party

To assess the cultural load in the semantic sense, list the vocabulary items that might cause problems. Say what students need to know about the cultural context in order to understand the vocabulary items you have listed.

Example:
good napkins   How are 'good napkins' different from 'napkins'?

Then, select and analyze the cultural load of another reading passage designed for students at a similar proficiency level as 'The Dinner Party'. Which text, the one shown below or your own, do you feel has a heavier cultural load? Why do you think so? In overseas teaching situations, what are the advantages of using texts with a light cultural load? What are the advantages of using ones with a heavy cultural load?

The Dinner Party

It is 7:55. The Smiths are coming to dinner at 8:00. Gina and Frank are not ready for the Smiths. They want everything to be perfect when the Smiths arrive. Mr. Smith is Frank's boss.

'Hurry, Frank, the Smiths are coming soon. We have to set the table. Bring in the dishes, please. I already have the bowls for the salad and the cups for the coffee. I don't have the knives, forks, and spoons. Bring those with the dishes. I have to put the tablecloth on the table and find the good napkins. Hurry, Frank there's so much to do!'

'I'm coming,' says Frank. Frank is carrying the dishes, the knives, the forks, and the spoons. He and Gina begin to set the table. Everything is ready. It is 8:00. At 8.01, the Smiths knock on the door. Gina and Frank answer the door together. They are ready for their perfect evening.

(DeFilippo and Skidmore 1984:113)

Note: In using this text, it would be important for teachers to make clear to students that in all societies there will be variance in what is acceptable social behavior depending on such things as age, social class, and ethnic background. Dinner parties can vary among members of the same society. One way teachers might illustrate this for students is to include another reading on a dinner party in which very different things occur.

2 In dealing with her students' desire to seek her advice on their personal problems, Veno-Kan explained to them that American teachers, while

happy to give advice on classroom questions, typically refer students to counselors to deal with personal problems.

What other solution could Veno-Kan have reached which might have better accommodated her students' desire to seek advice from her with the constraints on her time and her uncomfortableness in giving advice?

In discussing her problem in using group work in Japan, Veno-Kan reported that in order to get her students to pay less attention to one another when in groups, she encouraged them to get down to the task at hand by setting time limits on group work and giving extra points for completing the work on time; she also changed round the members of the groups.

What other approaches could Veno-Kan have taken to this problem? Can you think of any other options which would have incorporated her students' interest with one another into the group task itself?

In dealing with the attendance problem in her classes, Veno-Kan explained to her students the importance she placed on attendance and punctuality and penalized poor attendance and consistent lateness.

Suggest some other approaches that Veno-Kan could have taken which might have involved more accommodation on her part.

3 Burnaby and Sun (1989) in their investigation of Chinese teachers' view of western language teaching, comment as follows:

> Several of the teachers noted the strength of the traditional relationship in China between teachers and students, as well as the behaviors and teaching methods implied in this relationship. These strongly favor teacher-centered methods and structured curricula. . . . A few teachers expressed concerns, on their own part or those of their colleagues, about being influenced by fads in teaching methods. They mentioned that many of the activities common in communicative language teaching seemed like games rather than serious learning. Thus, some Chinese teachers feel that they are not really teaching when they use such activities, and they expect the students to complain about them.
>
> Several of the teachers commented favorably on the dynamic, creative and individualized approaches embodied in Western philosophies of education but noted that these approaches are difficult to apply in other cultural contexts: 'Culture gap. Chinese don't think in the way most Westerners think.' (Burnaby and Sun 1989:229)

Maley, cited earlier in the chapter, contends that:

> even now the most widely accepted view of learning in China is that it is memory-based. The teacher or textbook has the knowledge. (Maley 1986:104)

Given the traditional approach to learning in China, why do you think some Chinese teachers and learners view communicative language teaching as games and not serious learning? What would you do if some of the activities you used in class were viewed by the learners in this way?

4 In the article below, English (1989) discusses the cross-cultural problems she encountered in teaching English at the National University of Cote d'Ivoire. She describes two particular problems she was having with her students. First, they ignored her directions for group activities, adopting instead their usual behavior of copying down everything that was given in class. Second, her efforts to set up extracurricular activities were thwarted by her students' concern with passing the examination.

What action could English have taken to deal with both problems? How could she have accommodated the students' desire to copy things down with her own desire to have them become involved in activities without writing everything down? How might she have accommodated her own desire to involve students in extracurricular activities with her students' desire to pass their examination?

Teacher shock in Francophone Africa
by Susan Lewis English
National University of Cote d'Ivoire

When I first applied for a Fulbright Lecturing grant in TEFL/Applied Linguistics at the National University of Cote d'Ivoire (formerly the Ivory Coast), I knew which courses I would be teaching; yet I never guessed how much I would be learning. Now that I have passed the half-way mark in my 10-month assignment in Abidjan, I can begin to analyze my experience in terms of my cultural expectations, which might be called teacher shock.

Where's my class?
As I strode to my first class, a colleague stopped me on the sidewalk.

"Where were you this morning?" he asked. "The students were waiting for you."

"What do you mean? My class begins in 5 minutes."

"The time and place of the class were changed. Didn't you know?"

Five months later I am still jolted by unexpected variations in the class schedule. I am told, for example, to cancel classes to attend faculty meetings, which I may or may not know about in advance. The problem lies not with the English Department of the National University of Cote d'Ivoire but rather with my expectations about organization and management. Cross-cultural experts would say I suffer from high achievement motivation and low tolerance for ambiguity. Because I have specific goals in mind, I perceive every missed class as a threat to my achieving them. My Ivorian colleagues, who occasionally complain, accept sudden changes with relative ease.

Hurry up, please!

"Pass in your papers and open your books to page 61. Exercise B at the bottom. Number one. Kouame Andre? Not ready. Coulibaly Angeline? Kramako Victor?"

Five minutes later, Kouame Andre, Coulibaly Angeline, and about a third of the class are still passing in their papers and have not yet opened their books to page 61.

My professional goals are clear: to help as many students learn as much English in the shortest time possible. There are up to 60 students in each of my first-year composition classes. The semester allows for 26 weeks of instruction before the 2-month final exam period begins. Each class meets once a week. Therefore I have just 26 hours in which to affect my students' learning positively. I feel anxious when I consider what my students could be learning if only they would work more efficiently.

Americans are known for their future orientation, and I am no exception. To me, time is precious. Few of my Ivorian colleagues, however, seem to share my sense of urgency.

Don't write that down!

I write on the board:
1. Divide into groups of three.
2. One by one, read your essay aloud.
3. Listeners, tell to what extent you agree with the ideas stated.

I read the directions aloud, set a time limit, and give the signal to begin. As I work my way to the back of the room, I find few students actually performing the activity. Alternating red and blue ink, they are artfully copying the directions into their notebooks.

Copying is a classroom behavior my students have practiced daily for 15 years. The method by which middle school teachers check notebooks for correctness, completeness, and neatness is clearly specified by the Ministry of Education (*Guide Pratique*, 1984:27). A colleague of mine who is popular with his students says every sentence three times, making it easier for them to transcribe his words into their notebooks.

I, on the other hand, have come to Cote d'Ivoire with the idea of teacher as facilitator, a fashionable concept in ESL/EFL circles before I left the US. I want students to be active risk-takers who take responsibility for their learning. To remedy the situation, I turn to my bookshelf and browse through the section on teaching methodology. Titles like *Methods That Work* seem little more than wishful thinking.

Why can't we be friends?

"Since you teach at an all-girls' high school, you must have some interesting stories to tell," I commented to a young Frenchman doing alternate military service in Abidjan.
"What's there to tell?" he retorted. "I walk into class, give my lecture, and leave."

As an American, I don't want to just lecture and leave. I consider my students people rather than merely names in a roll book. I want to step down from my podium and create a sense of equality between me and the students. Besides, I have that typical American desire to be liked.

It is not surprising, though, that my attempts at extracurricular activities—starting an English table in the student cafeteria, opening a lending library in my office, meeting groups of students after class—have met with minimal response. There seems to be an invisible but unbreakable wall between the students and me. It is not built necessarily on respect, but rather on fear.

Their fear is well-founded. After final exams in June-July, about 50% of the first-year students and about 30% of the second-year students are expected to fail. Those who fail will have the option of retaking the exams in September-October. If they fail again, they may either repeat the year—without the necessary financial support—or drop out. These are the final steps in a weeding process that began for them at age 10: in 1979-80, when my students were in their early teens, the ratio of primary to university students in Cote d'Ivoire was approximately 89 to 1 (*Africa South of the Sahara*, 1986:18).

I find it difficult to accept this distance between students and teacher and the divisions that exist among the students themselves. Within a class, few students will, for example, share a book with someone outside their circle of friends unless specifically asked to do so. Cote d'Ivoire comprises many narrow in-groups as defined by family, ethnic origin, and socioeconomic status. The classroom, then, is a microcosm of Ivorian society in general.

However objective I have tried to be in summarizing my experience in Cote d'Ivoire, it is difficult to describe another educational system without showing ethnocentrism. Our beliefs about what education can and should be are formed during childhood and, for those of us who become professionals in the field, are further developed through work and advanced study. The debate we carry on in journals and at conferences is deceptive, for there is a consensus which underlies our discussions. It takes a cross-cultural encounter to challenge those beliefs.

(*TESOL Newsletter* 23/1:23)

Researching the ideas

1 As was pointed out in the chapter, a good deal of ethnographic research on minority education concludes that teachers' and learners' roles vary between different cultures. In order to gain a better understanding of these variations, research the topic of cross-cultural differences in minority education classrooms, focusing on the manner in which the learning that goes on *outside* the classroom in a particular culture or subculture affects the expectations of the teachers and/or students in the classroom. Two valuable sources to begin your research are the following:

Trueba, H.T., G.P. Guthrie, and K.H. Au. (eds.) 1981. *Culture and the Bilingual Classroom: Studies in Classroom Ethnography.* Rowley, Mass.:

Newbury House Publishers.

Trueba, H.T. (ed.) 1987. *Success of Failure? Learning and the Language Minority Student.* New York: Newbury House Publishers.

2 The chapter contains suggestions for undertaking some limited ethnographic research by employing what Damen calls *pragmatic ethnography.* Use elements taken from this model to learn more about the roles of teachers and students in a specific country, ideally a country in which you are considering working.

To begin, research available printed material on the roles of teachers and learners in the country. Then draw up an extensive list of questions you could ask informants from the country regarding the roles of teachers and students. Finally, interview at least three individuals regarding the roles of teachers and students. The following is a sample of the type of questions you might ask in the interviews.

The role of the teacher

a. Are teachers generally concerned about their students' family life and social life? If so, how do they show this interest?
b. Do teachers typically call their students by their first names in class?
c. Do teachers frequently socialize with their students, perhaps inviting them to their homes or out to eat in a restaurant?
d. Do teachers typically tell the students if they don't know the answer to a question?
e. What are common discipline problems teachers have, and how do they handle them?

The role of the learner

a. Do students frequently ask the teacher questions in class if they don't understand the material?
b. If students do not understand some class material, do they generally seek help from the teacher, either in class or out of class, from other students, or from either one?
c. Do students typically pick their own reading materials and writing topics?
d. Do students often study with one another?
e. Do students typically regard their personal responsibilities to their family and friends as more important than their school responsibilities?

Suggestions for further reading

Damen, L. 1987. *Culture Learning: The Fifth Dimension in the Language Classroom.* Reading, Mass.: Addison-Wesley Publishing.

Although this book is designed for training ESL teachers in the United States, the first section of the text presents a good introduction to the field of intercultural communication.

Trueba, H.T., G.P. Guthrie, and **K.H. Au.** (eds.) 1981. *Culture and the Bilingual Classroom: Studies in Classroom Ethnography.* Rowley, Mass.: Newbury House Publishers.
This book is a collection of microethnographic studies of minority children in American classrooms. The studies are relevant to overseas teaching situations in that they document cross-cultural differences in classroom behavior.

Valdes, J.M. (ed.) 1986. *Culture Bound.* Cambridge: Cambridge University Press.
This book includes theoretical and practical articles on the relationship between culture and the language classroom. Included are articles dealing with the relationship between language, thought, and culture, as well as those that deal specifically with teaching Middle Eastern and Chinese students.

PART TWO

The educational context

4 LANGUAGE TEACHING AND THE LANGUAGE EDUCATION CONTEXT

Theoretical background

Schools are the principal institutions for the implementation of the language-in-education policies referred to in Chapter 1; indeed, they are often viewed as primary agents for solving a whole host of social problems. This is particularly true in multilingual developing nations. As Santiago notes,

> Third World nations, particularly new states, have faced complex political, social and economic challenges in improving the quality of life of their citizenry. It is in the context of these complex and often conflicting if not competing interests that educational planning takes place. Much attention has been given the efforts but then much is expected of it in the form of societal returns. Schools are expected to engender feelings of nationalism, to enforce national language policies, to solve problems of social inequity, to solve problems of development and much more. (Santiago 1982:124)

The focus of this chapter is on the role of schools in carrying out national language-in-education policies. As was pointed out in Chapter 1, the decision as to which language or languages are given official status is made by the political leaders of a country. Once this decision is made, however, the implementation of this policy, in terms of education, is passed to another government agency, generally the Ministry or Department of Education. This body then makes several important decisions regarding the role of the chosen official language, or languages, in the schools.

First, the Ministry must decide what language to use as the medium of instruction in schools; if more than one language is designated, it must stipulate how each one is to be used, i.e. in which subjects or part of the day. It must further determine what language or languages will be studied as required subjects, and at what educational level and for how many hours each week these languages will be taught. It must also decide if it wishes to implement a standardized test of competency in the required languages.

A second area of official concern is the setting forth of curriculum guidelines, which typically specify language learning objectives and may specify textbook content. As was pointed out in Chapter 1, the Ministry of Education may direct a textbook commission of language specialists to design the classroom materials, but ultimately the materials must be approved by the Ministry itself. Once an overall curriculum is designed, the Ministry may sponsor in-service teacher training programs to familiarize teachers with the curriculum. It may also have inspectors who oversee the implementation of the stated curriculum by working with in-service teachers. Finally, if the question arises, the Ministry may address the issue of what variety of the language to promote in the schools.

While a Ministry of Education is instrumental in formulating the stated language policies of a country, it is important to recognize that there can be a significant discrepancy between a stated language policy and what is actually implemented. For example, while a Ministry may specify that a language of wider communication, like English, be used as the medium of instruction, if such a policy is not supported by factors in the educational context like trained teachers and adequate material resources, as well as by factors in the larger social context like economic incentives for knowing the language, it is quite unlikely that the stated policy will be successfully implemented. For this reason, stated policies must be examined within the political, economic, and educational contexts in which they exist.

In this chapter we will examine how the following decisions, made by Ministries of Education, affect the teaching of English in a country: the specification of a medium of instruction and required foreign languages; the specification of learning objectives, and the specification of a standard of language usage. To begin we will explore the issues involved in making each of these decisions, emphasizing the manner in which the stated policy and the implemented policy may be quite different. In the 'Case studies' section, we examine the effect that these decisions, as well as other educational and social factors, have on the quality of English teaching in three countries. Throughout the chapter we will discuss the implications of educational decisions for expatriate language teachers. First, we turn to an examination of the issues involved in implementing language policies in schools. These policies include both the choice of a medium of instruction and the choice of a language, or languages, as required subjects.

Language education policies

Medium of instruction

In multilingual nations, one of the major questions a Ministry of Education must address is the issue of what language to use as a medium of instruction. In many countries today, the sheer number of languages that exist make the question of the language of instruction a complex one. In India, for instance, some eighty languages are used as media of instruction in different regions and at different stages of education (Santiago 1982:116). As was pointed out in Chapter 1, one of the central areas of conflict in the designation of a medium of instruction is whether to provide initial education in the mother tongue or in a language of wider communication. Obviously this decision is related to which languages are given official recognition by political leaders and to the whole issue of nationalism versus nationism. However, even in A-modal nations, where a language of wider communication has been designated as the official language, a policy of mother tongue instruction in the primary schools may be advocated to ease the transition from the home to the wider society.

One of the most thorough and widely cited discussions of the advantages and disadvantages of mother tongue instruction occurred at the 1951 international meeting on the topic of vernacular languages in education sponsored by Unesco (the United Nations Educational, Scientific, and Cultural Organization). At the conference, a vernacular language was defined as 'a language which is the mother tongue of a group which is socially or politically dominated by another group speaking a different language' (Unesco 1953:689-90). In their final recommendation, Unesco urged support for vernacular education contending that

> the use of the mother tongue be extended to as late a stage in educa-
> tion as possible. In particular, pupils should begin their school
> through the medium of the mother tongue, because they understand
> it best and because to begin their school life in the mother tongue
> will make the break between home and school as small as possible.
> (Unesco 1953:691)

One common objection to vernacular education is that, since some languages have only an oral tradition and not a developed grammar or writing system, they cannot serve as a medium of instruction. Members of the Unesco meeting pointed out that there is nothing inherent in a language that precludes it from developing a writing system. Indeed Ferguson maintains that any language is amenable to linguistic develop-ment through corpus planning. This planning, however, must include three components: 'graphization—reduction to writing; standardization—

the development of a norm which overrides regional and social dialects; and, for want of a better term, modernization—the development of inter-translatability with other languages in a range of topics and forms of discourse characteristic of industrialized, secularized, structurally differentiated, "modern" societies' (Ferguson 1968:28). However, until such corpus planning is completed, and this demands considerable time and resources, vernacular languages which have only an oral tradition are not suitable media for instruction. In such instances, a language of wider communication, like English, may have to be selected as a medium of instruction.

Other objections have been made with regard to vernacular education. Some experts, for example, maintain that it could be used as a way of promoting the existing economic system by keeping the poor from acquiring the dominant language. This attitude, as was pointed out in Chapter 1, was held by many black South Africans when the Bantu education policy, which encouraged the use of vernacular education, was in force. Furthermore, some members of rural societies fear that the increased schooling made possible by vernacular education will lead to their young leaving the villages for urban areas and thus upset family earning patterns and life styles (Santiago 1982:128). Perhaps the most serious objections to vernacular education rest in very practical limitations touched on in the Unesco Report, namely lack of trained teachers, the lack of textbooks and general reading materials in the vernacular, and the inadequacy of the vernacular vocabulary to deal with some topics (Unesco 1953:692). The latter two objections demand a good deal of corpus planning to make the vernacular a viable educational tool.

As was pointed out in Chapter 1, the choice of which language to use as the medium of instruction is frequently made on the basis of political and social expediency rather than on that of educational effectiveness or feasibility. A language education policy may require students to learn more than one language in school, as in Cameroon with the learning of French and English. In such countries, children may spend a great deal of time learning a second or foreign language. In fact, Hartshone (1967) estimates that in South Africa, forty-five per cent of the day in Bantu schools is spent on language learning (as cited in Santiago 1982:129).

If students are required to learn many languages, it is unlikely that they will reach a high level of fluency in all of them. In cases where students and perhaps even the teachers are not fluent in a language of wider communication which has been designated as the medium of instruction, the primary language of the classroom may in fact be the vernacular. Thus, the stated policy concerning the medium of instruction may not in actuality be the implemented policy. What this suggests for expatriate language teachers is that knowing the language education policy of a country is not sufficient. In addition, they must examine how the policy is actually being implemented by doing such things as observing classes in the host country and discussing with local educators the state of language education.

In cases where one or more languages are designated as the medium of instruction, a Ministry of Education can issue guidelines as to how each language is to be used in schools. For example, in 1974, when the Philippines Department of Education and Culture mandated the use of English and Pilipino as media of instruction in the primary and secondary schools, it specified that English was to be used in English communication arts, mathematics, and science, while Pilipino was to be used in all other domains. One possible consequence of such a policy is that since students are to study particular subjects such as mathematics or science exclusively in one language, they will master the vocabulary of particular fields in only that language. However, it may be that in the implementation of the policy, a good deal of code-switching occurs in the classes, particularly if teachers and students are more fluent in one of the languages.

Required subject

In addition to designating the medium of instruction in schools, the Minstry of Education may designate one or more languages as required subjects of study. In designating a language as a required subject, the Minstry will typically specify at what level language instruction will begin and for how many hours each week. In some countries a language like English, while not a required subject, may be one of several possible choices to fulfill a foreign language requirement. The choice of which language to select may be left to the local school district or to individual students. Whether or not English is selected will depend on a variety of social, political, and economic factors. To the extent that English has the linguistic power that was referred to in Chapter 2, individuals may select it because they believe it will advance their own economic and social position.

A study of English education (Psychova 1975) in Czechoslovakia offers some insight into why individuals may select English as their foreign language. In Czechoslovakia, when Psychova carried out her study, students could select English, French, or German as their second foreign language, with Russian as their first. Among gymnasium students in an industrial district in Ostrava, English had the highest preference rating (65.9 per cent), followed by German (27.8 per cent), and then French (6.3 per cent). In terms of why students selected the language they did, the reasons given were similar for all three languages. The most frequent reasons were: a need for personal communication with foreigners, especially when travelling abroad; and a need for reading and under-standing special (scientific) literature. However, the choice of English was often motivated by the popularity of the language created through pop-music, films, etc.' (Pyschova 1975, as cited in Prucha 1985:7). The widespread use of English in the mass media may be a significant factor in promoting study of the language among young people, and class materials which take this into account may well increase student motivation.

In cases where English is designated as a required second language, or even as an option, the Ministry of Education may institute a standardized test of language proficiency. The case studies at the end of the chapter illustrate the effect of such examinations on student motivation and the teaching curriculum.

Implications for language teaching

If you are teaching in a country where English is one of the designated media of instruction it is important to investigate several issues. First, at what stage is it introduced? In some countries, such as South Africa, initial instruction is in the mother tongue with English introduced later in the primary program. By knowing at what level and in what manner the transition is made, you can better predict your students' proficiency in English at various ages.

Second, if there is more than one language designated as the medium of instruction, you will need to find out how the various languages are used in the curriculum. Is English, as in the Philippines, used as a medium of instruction in particular fields of study? An answer to this question will provide you with a basis for making some predictions about your students' familiarity with the vocabulary of various fields of study. Finally, and most importantly, you will need to investigate if the official policy of using English as a medium of instruction actually reflects what is happening in the schools. For example, Platt *et al.* (1984:17) point out that in many West African nations, while the official medium is English, the actual medium used is Krio, Pidgin, or local languages. In situations like this, where policy does not reflect reality, you may find your students are much less proficient in English than you expected.

If you are working in a country where English is a required or optional subject of study it is important to find out the level at which students begin studying the language and the number of hours of instruction per week, both of which provide information for making predictions about fluency. Knowing whether or not there is a required foreign language competency exam, and the significance of this exam for students' further study, will provide you with a better understanding of students' motivation for learning English. While it is extremely important to examine the stated language education policy in a country, as mentioned above, there can be a significant difference between the stated policy and what actually happens in the classroom. Factors such as the number of required languages, the training of teachers, and the amount of material resources will all affect whether or not a stated language policy is fully implemented.

Curriculum guidelines

Learning objectives

A second policy area dealt with by Ministries or Departments of Education is the specification of curriculum guidelines. How detailed the objectives are varies greatly from country to country. In South Africa, for example, the Department of Education and Training provides a detailed curriculum for each grade level with specific objectives listed for each of the skill areas. For instance, in Standard Five, when English is first used as the medium of instruction, students are expected to master the following listening skills:

> **Aural** (the listening skill)
> Pupils must be exposed to a variety of listening activities which should include at least the following:
> 1. Minimal pairs practice: discriminating between words which sound similar in fluent spoken English, for example, *still, steal; much, march; course, cause, coarse; pin, pen; lead, lid.*
> 2. Following instructions and commands so as to carry them out.
> 3. Recognizing the way in which the voice is used (stress, intonation, etc.) to express subtleties in meaning, for example, *What...! What! What?* and the different variations of meaning through switches in emphasis:
> *I* know the place.
> I *know* the place.
> I know *the* place.
> I know the *place.*
> 4. Recognizing how speakers, or people reading aloud are
> – introducing or developing an idea
> – emphasizing a point
> – illustrating a point
> – changing a line of thought
> – drawing a conclusion.
> A paragraph or other passage of limited length is to be used as a base for developing these skills.
> 5. Listening to oral presentations (e.g. lessons, talks, newscasts, interviews) so as to be able to distinguish main ideas, arguments and fact, and so as to take notes.
> Passages of limited length are to be used to develop these skills.

Recorded texts by a range of speakers (including both first and second language speakers) are indispensable.

6. Following the argument in conversations, small group discussions and debates, so as to be able to participate in them.

7. Recognizing different social situations (formal and informal) and relationships (peer group; older-younger persons; polite/rude tone toward subordinates) suggested by different choices of words, idiom and register.

(South African Department of Education and Training, *Syllabus for English Standard Five*. 1986:2–3)

Since students are evaluated on the basis of this curriculum at the end of the year, both teachers and students have a strong motivation to adhere to the curriculum objectives.

At times, however, the stated curriculum will not reflect what is actually occurring in the classroom. This discrepancy may be due to a variety of factors. One reason may be that students do not have the linguistic competence to deal with the objectives set forth in the guidelines. Chitravelu (1985:19), for example, points out that most teachers in Malaysia find that the majority of their students do not have the language proficiency necessary to deal with the communicative tasks specified in the curriculum. Chitravelu believes that the reason the curriculum does not match the proficiency level of the students is that 'curriculum innovation and change is always initiated from the top in Malaysia' (ibid.:20) and there is little consultation with in-service teachers. In addition, the Ministry of Education provides little help to teachers in terms of showing them how to implement the curriculum, a factor which, as we shall see in the 'Case studies' section, greatly affects the quality of English teaching.

Another possible reason for a discrepancy between a stated and implemented curriculum is that it may include more objectives than can feasibly be taught in the specified time period. This is true in Malaysia where Chitravelu (ibid.:19) maintains that the fact that many teachers believe that the curriculum is 'overloaded' has 'given rise to a major preoccupation among most teachers to "cover the syllabus" rather than to teach effectively at the level of capability of the students. . . . Teachers, therefore, often select only those skills that feature prominently in examinations.'

In some cases teachers feel compelled to cover a syllabus because they believe they will be judged by Ministry of Education language inspectors on the basis of how well they adhere to a curriculum and how well their students do on examinations which are based on the syllabus. Frequently, the implementation of a curriculum can result in a good deal of conflict between teachers and Ministries of Education. Chitravelu, in reference to the Malaysian context, explains this conflict in the following way:

> Ministry officials claim that their stand is that any syllabus is only a guide, the fare for the theoretical 'average student' which has to be interpreted and adapted to get the best pedagogic fit for the specified set of students a teacher teaches. Teachers claim the Ministry demands that they 'cover the syllabus' but Ministry officials quip, 'If you want to cover the syllabus, use brown paper.' (Chitravelu 1985:21)

What such statements suggest is that obtaining the curriculum guidelines for a country, while necessary, is not sufficient. In order to gain an understanding of what is actually being taught in the schools, you will need to study the issue much more carefully by doing such things as questioning local teachers regarding their views on the curriculum, finding out if the Ministry has undertaken projects to help teachers explore ways of implementing the curriculum, and observing classes.

Curriculum objectives such as those provided by the South African Department of Education and Training represent one end of the continuum. They are, as the example demonstrates, quite specific, and since they provide the basis for the year-end evaluation often for both students and teachers, a good deal of energy is devoted to 'covering' them. At the other end of the continuum is the situation in which no set syllabus or texts are provided, one which, in most countries, is more typical of private institutions, and those of higher learning, than of state run primary and secondary schools.

Balhorn and Schneider (1987) experienced a lack of curriculum objectives in their teaching position as EFL instructors at a Korean university. As native speakers of English, they were asked to teach a communicatively oriented course rather than one of the more typical courses in literary criticism, linguistics, or pedagogy. They were given complete freedom to determine the syllabus, text, and content of the course. Indeed, they found that many expatriate EFL teachers, like themselves, had been hired to teach communicative courses, and had been given complete freedom to design their own syllabus. Unfortunately, they had been provided with little information on which to base their decisions. As they say,

> It is not uncommon for an EFL teacher to be hired in the morning, select a textbook in the afternoon and begin the first class of the semester the following day. More importantly, no information about the students is available. Direct questions in regard to what the students have studied previously, what they will study subsequently, what their needs are or what the goals of the class are, are all met with what to American and British language teachers are vague and indirect responses. Oftentimes, there seems to be little coherence or continuity to the program. As responsibility for the communicative

curriculum was very likely solely that of the previous EFL teacher, any structure or continuity that may have existed has left the program when the previous teacher departed and the new one came in. (Balhorn and Schneider 1987:15)

Given the problems that can result from having no standardized curriculum, they argue that what is needed in a teaching situation like their own is for the 'permanent Korean faculty to establish goals, construct a program, and inform and/or train incoming teachers, for without this kind of organization, the untrained or perhaps less than conscientious ESL instructors have little effect on the communicative proficiency of the students' (ibid.). However, as we shall see below, there are some disadvantages in having a specified curriculum.

Implications for language teaching

There are several disadvantages to working in a setting where curriculum objectives are clearly specified and centrally controlled. First, as was pointed out in the discussion on Malaysia, in this kind of context it may be more difficult to meet the needs of the learners. The fact that teachers are supposed to adhere to set objectives may make them less inclined to undertake any needs analysis, as they feel that they have no authority to modify the curriculum to meet specific needs. Thus, in their role as teachers, they may do little more than carry out the requirements of the curriculum. As Nunan (1988:21) points out, in situations where a government department or agency designs a curriculum and then disseminates it to a wide range of learning institutions, the responsibility of the teacher is 'often little more than to implement the curriculum and to act as "classroom manager".' Another potential disadvantage of set curricula is that often they specify *what* is to be learned, but not *how* it is to be learned. For example, while the South African listening objectives set out on pages 85–6 specify that students are expected to master the skill of 'recognizing different social situations and relationships,' they do not indicate how this is to be taught or assessed. Thus, what actually occurs in the classroom may or may not meet the specified objectives.

There are, however, several advantages to having a curriculum, particularly one that is carefully designed and field tested. First, it provides continuity from one level to the next so that teachers have some way of determining what exposure their students have had to English. Second, the objectives can provide a framework within which staff members can work together to design activities and tasks. Nunan (1988:36) notes that because curriculum planners have assumed that 'planning equals teaching equals learning,' they have tended to focus on the planned and assessed curriculum rather than the implemented curriculum. However, the existence of a planned curriculum allows teachers to focus on the implemented curriculum as they discuss ways to best achieve the objectives of the curriculum in their particular institution.

The varieties of English

A final area which Ministries of Education may address is the question of what variety of English to promote in the curriculum, the local variety or one used in an anglophone country. As was pointed out in Chapter 1, in countries like the Philippines and India, where English has official status and is widely used in the society, new varieties of English have developed. Because of this, Ministries of Education, when approving classroom materials and training teachers, must decide what variety of English to advocate. Again, it is important to remember that there may be discrepancies between the stated and the implemented policy. While the Ministry may advocate the use of a variety of English spoken in an anglophone country, what is actually used in the classroom may be a local variety, or what is sometimes described as a 'New English'. We turn now to a discussion of what is meant by 'New Englishes' and the implications of such varieties for the expatriate teacher.

A definition of New Englishes

Kachru points out that speakers of English can be viewed from three perspectives:

> that of a native user for whom English is the first language in almost all functions [the inner circle]; that of a non-native user who considers English as a foreign language and uses it in highly restricted domains [the expanding circle]; and that of a non-native user who uses an institutionalized second-language variety of English [the outer circle]. (Kachru 1986:19)

Table 4.1 (overleaf) illustrates these three types of situations with the inner circle representing native users of English, the outer circle representing speakers of an institutionalized variety of English, and the expanding circle representing non-native speakers who use English as a foreign language.

What Kachru terms an 'institutionalized second language variety' arises when a society makes use of English on a day-to-day basis along with one or more other languages. According to Kachru (1986:19), by having a large range of functions in a society over a long period of time, institutionalized varieties of English develop unique features.

Platt, Weber, and Lian (1984:2–3) describe what Kachru calls an institutionalized second language variety as a New English and outline the following characteristics. First, a New English develops through the educational structure where it is used either as a medium of instruction or taught as a subject. Second, it develops in an area where a native variety of English is not spoken by most of the population. Third, it is used for a variety of functions within the area in which it is spoken. And finally, a New English has become localized or nativized by adopting some language features that are unique to the region.

The inner circle	The outer circle	The expanding circle
	e.g.	*e.g.*
Australia	Bangladesh	China
Canada	Ghana	Egypt
New Zealand	India	Indonesia
UK	Kenya	Israel
USA	Malaysia	Japan
	Nigeria	Korea
	Pakistan	Nepal
	Philippines	Saudi Arabia
	Singapore	Taiwan
	Sri Lanka	USSR
	Tanzania	Zimbabwe
	Zambia	

Table 4.1: The three concentric circles of English (adapted from Kachru 1989:86)

A New English functions as what Smith (1983:14) calls an *intranational* language, i.e. 'a language, other than the mother tongue, which is used by nationals of the same country for communication.' Smith contrasts this with an *international* language which 'is used by people of different nations to communicate with one another.' In countries of the inner and outer circles English is used as both an intranational and an international language, while in countries of the expanding circle it is used only as an international language.

Platt *et al.* (1984:6–7) maintain that New Englishes can arise in three types of contexts. First, a New English can develop in an area where young people receive education in English having had little or no previous exposure to the language in their homes. This might occur in some regions of the Philippines or India. Second, a New English can arise in countries like Ghana or Sierra Leone where children often come to school already knowing an English-based pidgin. (A *pidgin* is a simplified language variety often used as a lingua franca for commercial purposes.) Finally, a New English can develop in countries like Jamaica or Trinidad where children frequently come to school knowing an English-based creole. (A *creole* is a language variety which develops from a pidgin. It is syntactically more complex and is used within a society for a wider range of purposes, often including most of the communication of everyday life.)

Characteristics of New Englishes

A great deal has been written on the actual features that distinguish a particular New English like Indian English or Singapore English. (See the 'Suggestions for further reading' for a list of selected readings.) The following are just some examples of the kinds of features which exist on the phonological, syntactic, lexical, and discourse levels.

Suprasegmental and phonological features Speakers of Singapore English do not use stress distinctions to mark different parts of speech. Thus, in Singapore English 'increase' and 'object' would be pronounced as 'in*crease*' and 'ob*ject*' when used either as a verb or a noun (Tay 1982:61). In Nigerian English, the dental fricatives /θ/ and /ð/ are realized by some speakers as [t] and [d] (Jibril 1982:76).

Morphological and syntactic features In Nigerian English, many non-count nouns like 'information' and 'equipment', are pluralized (Jibril 1982:78). In Singapore English, some speakers employ a specific word order in indirect questions using sentences like 'May I ask where is the stamp counter?' (Tay 1982:63). Because such constructions are frequently used by individuals who are in the process of learning English, currently there is a debate among linguists as to whether or not New Englishes are basically a type of *interlanguage* (i.e. comparable to the language spoken by learners before they develop full competence). For a discussion of some of the issues involved in this debate, see Lowenberg 1986b and Davies 1989.

Lexical features Several processes can be involved in the coining of new words in New Englishes. In some cases new words are added to the language by borrowing local terms and incorporating them into English. For example, in Nigerian English the Yoruba word '*danfo*' is used to refer to a tiny uncomfortable bus, and '*buka*' is used to describe a small roofed enclosure that exists by a roadside for selling food. Other words are added to a New English by combining an English term with a local one. For instance, in Indian English speakers can refer to '*janta meals*', '*lathi charge*', and '*tiffin carrier*' ('*janta*' meaning the people or masses, '*lathi*' being a long iron tipped stick to control crowds, and '*tiffin*' being a snack or light meal) (Kachru 1986:42).

New words are also added through semantic innovation or *calques*. In these instances, while the words are in English, they are being used in a manner that is consistent with the lending language. For example, in

Nigerian English one will hear the expression 'next tomorrow' for the more standard 'day after tomorrow'. This is a translation from the Yoruba '*otunla*' meaning 'new tomorrow' (Jibril 1982:81). Also in Nigerian English one will hear the expression 'We'll wash it!' when someone breaks some good news to friends. This is based on the Yoruba expression to 'wash' a happy event with drinks (ibid.:81).

Finally, words and expressions can be added to New Englishes by extending the meaning of standard English expressions. Thus, for example, in Nigerian English a 'drop' can mean the longest distance that a passenger can travel for the minimum taxi fare (ibid.:83).

Discourse features New Englishes often exemplify different rhetorical styles based on the discourse and rhetorical patterns of the local language. For example, Kachru (1986:44) cites an opening from a personal letter in South Asian English which begins very differently from a typical personal letter in an anglophone country. 'I am quite well here hoping the same for you by virtue of mighty God. I always pray to God for your good health, wealth and prosperity.' Death announcements also reflect local rhetorical expectations. For instance, in the *Hindustan Times*, they typically speak of 'the sad demise' or 'the sudden and untimely demise' of individuals who have 'left for heavenly abode' (ibid.:44).

Reasons for the continued use of New Englishes

New Englishes develop and continue to exist for a variety of reasons. Jibril, in his discussion of Nigerian English, points out that internal pressures preserve the continued use of a particular variety of English in Nigeria:

> First, there is pressure from the mother tongue, with its own set of rules which are often in conflict with those of English and upon which the Nigerian learner of English frequently falls back. There is also pressure from Pidgin English with its deceptive similarity to English. Then there is pressure from the complexity of English itself —its misleading spelling, hybrid vocabulary, and eccentric preposi- tions, all of which defy complete mastery. And this situation is not helped by the Nigerian teacher of English, who is more often than not a literature graduate to whom the English language is nothing but a beautiful grand mystery. Finally, there is pressure from society —the kind of English the Nigerian learner reads in newspapers and in locally written textbooks, and the kind of English he hears from everyone around him. (Jibril 1982:82–3)

These factors could all work to undermine a stated language education policy that promotes a variety of English used in the 'inner circle'. The only factor mentioned above that the educational context has any control over is English teacher training. As we shall see in the 'Case studies' section, if a Ministry of Education chooses to give little attention to this area, the quality of English teaching will suffer. However, even with a strong teacher training program, it is important to recognize that the variety of English used in a country is not, and cannot be, completely controlled by the educational context. Factors which are part of the larger social and linguistic context will play a significant role in this matter.

Perhaps one of the most important reasons for the continued use of Nigerian English is the attitude of Nigerians toward 'inner circle' varieties of English. Jibril (ibid.:83) maintains that Nigerians do not place a high value on imitating an 'inner circle' variety. In fact, 'the cultural climate in Nigeria at the present time discourages any tendency towards a perfect, native-like accent, though there is no corresponding aversion to impeccable written English.' The fact that Nigerians do not wish to acquire an 'inner circle' accent, although they strive for standard written English, raises the question of what variety of English should be taught in countries where a New English exists.

The question of varieties

In 1968, Prator argued strongly for English teachers throughout the world to promote an 'inner circle' variety of English. While listing various arguments for his position, he maintained that the strongest argument for using an 'inner circle' variety in the classroom is that

> if teachers in many different parts of the world aim at the same stable, well documented model, the general effects of their instruction will be convergent; the speech of their pupils will become more and more similar to that of pupils in many other regions, and the area within which communication is possible will grow progressively larger. If many diverse models are chosen, however, and once concession to regionalism leads to ever further concessions, the overall effect is bound to be divergent. Widespread intercomprehensibility will be lost with no guaranteed corresponding gain in local intelligibility. (Prator 1968:469)

Prator's perspective reflects what Kachru (1982:49-50) terms a *monomodel* approach to World Englishes; this model assumes that there is a single, homogeneous English second language community and that the functional roles assigned to English and the goals for studying it are more or less the same in all countries. Kachru contrasts this model with a *polymodel* approach which assumes that there is great variability in the use of English related to proficiency level and context. According to Kachru, in order for an institutionalized variety of English to be accepted in a country, 'the users must demonstrate a solidarity, an identity and a loyalty toward the language variety' (1986:50). A study by Shaw (1983) suggests that English speakers in the 'outer circle' countries are increasingly supporting their own varieties of English.

Shaw (1983) investigated the attitudes of college-educated speakers of English toward various models of English in India, Singapore, and Thailand. A large percentage of those polled (40 per cent or more) in all three countries believed that there was a unique variety of English spoken in their country. However, while only 3.5 per cent of the Thais felt that their variety of English should be taught in the schools, 47.7 per cent of the Indians, and 38.9 per cent of the Singaporeans felt that their local variety should be the model. While in all countries support for the use of a local variety was under 50 per cent, in the two countries (India and Singapore) where English has official status and is widely used, support for the local variety was much larger than in Thailand. This would suggest that in countries where English is spoken on a day-to-day basis, not only is a unique variety developing but more and more speakers in such countries are beginning to consider the local variety as the acceptable model for teachers to use.

Literary figures in many countries also support the use of a local variety of English. For example,

> the Malaysian writer K.S. Mamian reports that 'we used to honour the language (English) because we honoured our former rulers. Now we have come to a cutoff point. English will still be learned but it will be spoken in a different way. Our way' (*Asiaweek*, 10/1/82:40). Similarly, the renowned African writer Chinua Achebe feels that 'the English language will be able to carry weight with its ancestral home but altered to suit its new African surroundings' (in Ikara, 1981:3). Concerning Indian English, Subrahmanian (1977:24) agrees with Achebe: 'The language we use is English; the way we use it should be our own, though it may not be to the liking of the English'. (as cited in Lowenberg 1986a:11)

The problem of what variety of English to teach includes not only the question of what phonological and grammatical standards to use, but also the question of what standards of appropriateness to apply. Kramsch (1987) contends that since many aspects of spoken language are culturally determined, teachers need to teach both rules of grammar and rules of appropriateness in order for their students to achieve communicative competence. She suggests two ways that language use can be taught in a classroom. First, teachers can 'serve as social models in the classroom and diversify their interaction styles to include natural discourse patterns' (ibid.:247). Thus, teachers might try to incorporate in their speech a variety of forms for expressing such things as asking for clarification, indicating that they are listening, and starting and ending conversations. Second, teachers can encourage more interactional tasks in the classroom by making use of small groups, problem-solving tasks, and debates and discussions. These encourage students to use language appropriately to interrupt one another and claim the chance to speak (ibid.:248).

In contexts where English is used primarily as an international language between non-native speakers, it is difficult to know what standard of language appropriateness should be applied: the rules of speaking of an anglophone country or the rules of speaking of the countries from which the speakers come. In other words, if a Japanese and an Indonesian businessman are interacting in English in Singapore, whose standard of appropriateness should be applied—Japanese, Indonesian, Singaporean, or American or British? The issue then of varieties is a complex one which entails questions of phonological and grammatical accuracy, as well as those of linguistic appropriateness.

Implications for language teachers

What variety of English should expatriate language teachers promote? Perhaps the best answer to this question is offered by Strevens (1987:62) when he says: 'First, you teach the kind of English you use. . . . Second, teach as well—i.e. with as much professionalism—as you can.' At the same time, expatriate language teachers need to be sensitive to the desires of local leaders. This is particularly true in reference to spoken English. Ultimately, as Hill (1982:242) notes, 'teachers—particularly native English speakers working in developing countries—should always be aware of the wider implication of what they are teaching, tread sensitively and realize that English is not merely a neutral instrument of communication.'

What variety of English local teachers should employ is more problematic. For example, in parts of West Africa, even in the face of government opposition, some primary teachers use Pidgin English. As one primary teacher in Cameroon points out, 'For the first six months I have to use Pidgin. If I didn't, the children would not understand *one word.* Only after I have trained them in Pidgin can I begin to use proper English' (as cited in Platt *et al.* 1984:16). Tay (1982), in reference to the situation in Singapore, argues that teachers must evaluate the variety that is used on the basis of the context in which it is used. As she says, teachers 'should not condemn features of the basilect as substandard or uneducated, but point out that they may be used not only among the uneducated but also by the educated if they wish to mark the dimensions of informality, rapport, solidarity and intimacy' (Tay 1982:68). Native teachers then may have sound reasons for promoting local varieties in the classroom, reasons which arise from matters of intelligibility and social solidarity.

The existence of varieties of English may cause you to have problems both with understanding your students and in being understood by them. At times you will need to seek clarification from your students as to what they mean, and, in turn, to teach them ways of seeking clarification when they do not understand you. In addition, it is important to be aware that the local variety can be a basis for social solidarity. Thus, even if the educational context, in its materials and policies, supports an 'inner circle' variety, there will be strong pressures on the students to use the local variety.

There are a number of different factors which interplay with one another in determining the quality and extent of English teaching in schools (and institutions of higher education). For example, in the sociopolitical context the issue of nationalism can promote negative attitudes toward the learning of English. In the educational context the amount of money which governments appropriate to language teaching influences such things as teaching load and teacher training programs. Decisions made by Ministries of Education regarding the designation of a medium of instruction, required foreign languages, competency exams, curriculum objectives, and standards of usage are also factors which will affect the role of English in educational institutions. Another important factor is teacher training. In some countries Ministries of Education take an active role in promoting in-service teacher training projects in order to make teachers aware of new language training methods and materials, while in others this area may be neglected.

We turn now to a discussion of the role of English in the language education policies of three countries in order to analyze how all of the factors listed above affect English teaching in the country. The case studies illustrate three different official roles that English can have in a school system: as a compulsory second language, as a co-medium of instruction, and as an elective foreign language.

Case studies

English as a required subject: Malaysia

As was pointed out in Chapter 1, although English was at one time the medium of instruction in Malaysia, the 1967 Language Policy prescribed that it should be gradually phased out. The issues of what variety of English to teach, what cultural content to include, and what language to use as the medium of instruction have all been affected by the strong nationalist sentiment that currently exists in Malaysia. First, as a result of the country's history, a distinct institutionalized variety of Malaysian English exists. (For a full discussion of the features of Malaysian English, see Augustin 1982.) Although the schools have no policy on the use of this variety, those who support the development of a national identity tend to favor the promotion of Malaysian English. Second, as far as the cultural content of the curriculum is concerned, the general trend within the educational structure is to restrict the use of English to business and scientific domains and in this way to keep the cultural load of teaching texts to a minimum. Finally, with regard to the medium of instruction, again as a way of promoting a national identity, Malaysia has a policy of Malay-medium education with English introduced as a compulsory subject. Against this general framework, let us examine the role of English in Malaysian language policy and suggest how this is likely to affect the work of expatriate language teachers.

Various policy documents provide insight into the current objectives of English language education in Malaysia. For example, a recent Cabinet Committee Report states that the main objectives for learning English are '(1) to enable pupils to use the English language in certain jobs and activities, and (2) for a small group, to enable them to increase their skills in the language so that they can use the language for specific purposes in tertiary education' (as cited in Chitravelu 1985:10-11). Such objectives reflect a predominantly instrumental motivation to learn English.

Among some Malaysians, there is a desire to see that English, as Fishman (1982:16) puts it, 'stays in its place' and does not compete with Bahasa Malaysia. For example, Asmah, a Malaysian sociolinguist, argues that

> if English is given equality with the national language in the system of education, the latter language will stand to lose in terms of its development. From the sociological aspect of language development, the national language if left to a 'second-class' citizenship will have very little chance of being used in the teaching and writing of works of a highly intellectual and academic nature. (Asmah, as cited in Chitravelu 1985:85)

The aspect of language education policy which chiefly supports this desire to restrict the use of English is its designation as a compulsory school subject rather than as a medium of instruction. In contrast to its previous use as a medium of instruction, the number of hours now set aside for English in the curriculum is quite modest. Currently English is taught as a second language in all national primary schools beginning in the first year, while in all Chinese and Tamil primary schools, English as a third language is introduced into the curriculum in the third year. Thus, in Chinese and Tamil schools, students must learn two additional languages, Bahasa Malaysia and English. Although the number of hours of English instruction increases through primary school, the actual time allotted for

English instruction throughout the entire school system never exceeds five hours per week (Chitravelu 1985:11-14).

In addition to these restrictions, English teaching in Malaysia is being weakened by problems in student motivation, attitudes toward the curriculum and methodology, and teacher training.

Motivation

Students are not highly motivated to learn English since they need only take, and are not obliged to pass, an English language examination in the fifth year of primary school. Furthermore, especially in rural areas, English is rarely heard outside the classroom. Hence, there is neither instrumental nor integrative motivation to learn the language.

Curriculum and methodology

As was mentioned earlier, many teachers feel that they must cover the stated syllabus, even though Ministry officials may claim that it is only a guide which needs to be interpreted and adapted. Still, teachers believe that they have little freedom to modify the syllabus since 'the topics to be covered in a year are listed in a sequence and the sequence in which the syllabus spells out the linguistic items is plaster-cast by schools as the sequence in which the items have to be taught' (Chitravelu 1985:20). Given this attitude, teachers aim only to cover the syllabus rather than to assess the needs and interests of their students and design activities to meet them. This in itself is likely to reduce student motivation.

The methods used to implement the curriculum in schools tend to be very traditional. Although Malaysia was one of the pioneers in developing communicative language teaching materials, little was done to prepare the schools for the necessary changes in methodology. Few teacher training courses were offered, no appropriate textbooks were made available, nor was class size reduced to provide more suitable conditions for the communicative approach. As a consequence, few teachers have implemented the stated policy of adopting communicative teaching methods (ibid.:21). The fact that there is a discrepancy between stated policy and what actually happens in Malaysian classrooms demonstrates how the successful enactment of language policies requires a good deal of support from a Ministry of Education in terms of such things as classroom materials and teacher education.

Teacher training

A good many teachers of English in Malaysia are not English majors. In fact, in some areas, only one-sixth of the teachers have a degree in the subject. In some cases, teachers who have never gone through an English course or taught the language before are compelled to teach it (ibid.:24). This situation is in marked contrast to the stated language education policy which requires teachers to have an English degree, and provides a further instance of a discrepancy between stated and implemented policies.

The current situation in Malaysia favors only those who wish to restrict or even eliminate the use of English. The recent designation of English as a 'strong second language' rather than as an 'official language' has clearly had its effect on student motivation and demonstrates that when a language suffers a reduction in status the quality of instruction will tend to suffer.

Expatriate English teachers who take up posts in a country like Malaysia, where the language generally has little status, can expect the following. First, they are likely to find themselves teaching students who have neither integrative motivation to use the language nor instrumental motivation to pass an examination. Second, many local teachers are likely not to be highly proficient in English. Because of this, while some may be eager to interact with native speakers and thus improve their English, others may be very reluctant to interact with them for fear of revealing their lack of fluency. Finally, given what teachers perceive as a rigidly controlled language syllabus, many will be unwilling to modify their approach and materials to meet the needs of their students; indeed in some instances they will be insufficiently trained to do so.

English as a medium of instruction: The Philippines

The Philippines contrasts in several ways with Malaysia. English is still a medium of instruction, but the Philippines seems to be moving toward a situation similar to that in Malaysia in which Pilipino will be promoted to develop a national identity with English having a much more restricted role. Historically, the role of English in Filipino education has undergone several transformations. After the United States took over the Philippines from Spain in 1898, English was the sole medium of instruction in schools. In 1957 the vernacular was made the medium of instruction in Grades 1 and 2, with English and Pilipino as subjects; from Grade 3 on English was the medium of instruction with Pilipino as an auxiliary language. In 1974 a bilingual education policy was adopted in which Pilipino became the medium of instruction in social studies, character education, work education, and health and physical education with English used in English arts, science, and math (Galang 1988:236–7). This is the policy currently in effect in the schools.

As in Malaysia, the desire to promote a national identity is affecting the variety of English and the cultural content that is used in the schools. At the present time there appears to be support for using Filipino English. As Otanes points out,

> the variety of English that we should try to have our learners achieve mastery of is not, as previously advocated, one that is a close imitation of a native-speaker variety, like the one spoken in the United States or Britain. This, we have found out through years of drilling in pronunciation, is in fact a near-impossible feat, except for those whom we might call geniuses in language learning. . . . For Filipinos learning English, a more modest goal should be set—that of being able to speak a variety that is internationally understood and accepted. This is the variety already spoken by educated Filipinos from all ethnic groups and linguistic areas. (Otanes 1988:84)

In terms of the cultural content of the curriculum, as was pointed out in Chapter 3, curriculum developers in the Philippines are presently designing texts based on the local culture. Thus, there does not seem to be widespread support for cultural materials from abroad.

While the Philippines shares with Malaysia a desire to promote a national identity and perhaps eventually to replace English in the schools with Pilipino, the current state of English teaching in the Philippines is quite different from that in Malaysia in terms of student motivation, curriculum implementation, and teacher training. Unlike Malaysia, all three factors are strengthening rather than weakening the quality of teaching.

Motivation

Students who live in the Manila area where English is widely used have a real need to become fluent in the language, particularly for communication in formal domains. This is not the case on some of the other islands and in rural areas where English is not nearly as widely used. However, the fact that the college entrance examination is mainly in English provides an incentive for students from all areas to gain proficiency in the language. This situation contrasts sharply with Malaysia where neither integrative nor instrumental motivation is high.

Curriculum

The Ministry of Education, Culture, and Sports is working actively to improve the writing of textbooks and their distribution. The Ministry distributes outlines called Minimum Learning Competencies which specify what should be included in textbooks. (See the 'Exploring the ideas' section at the end of this chapter for an example of such a guideline.) These competencies are then sent to the Instruction Material Corporation which organizes a competition in the writing of textbooks (Sibayan 1985:53–4). Under the current system, there is competitive adoption of textbooks from various sources, including commercially produced texts and an in-service teacher training program which shows teachers how to use the textbooks. (Otanes 1988:85). Thus, unlike Malaysia, more leeway is given for the development of curriculum objectives and teacher training is supported as an integral part of curriculum ·adoption. The inclusion of a teacher training component increases the chances that teachers will not just cover the curriculum but seek to meet the particular needs of their students within its general framework.

Teacher training

Concern over what educational leaders view as the 'deterioration' of English proficiency among teachers and supervisors resulted in a national conference in 1979 on the state of English teaching. This conference led to several measures to improve the situation, including annual national seminar-workshops for English teachers, as well as scholarships to send classroom teachers and supervisors to local universities to take in-service courses. In contrast to Malaysia, the Ministry of Education, along with local universities, is taking an active role to improve the quality of teaching. In this way, while some in the Philippines would prefer to see the use of English restricted, the Ministry, through its active involvement in teacher training, is helping to promote high quality English teaching which will only contribute to the spread of the language. The situation in the Philippines illustrates how the language education context can operate to counteract the goals of the sociopolitical context, at least the goals of those who wish to see English replaced with Pilipino.

Expatriate language teachers who accept a job in a country like the Philippines, where English is used as a medium of instruction and where there is a great deal of government and university support for upgrading the quality of teaching, can make certain predictions about their jobs. First, because of the widespread use of English in society and in higher education, their students are likely to be quite motivated to learn the language both for instrumental and integrative reasons. Second, because of the widespread emphasis on teacher training, expatriate language teachers are more likely to find local teachers who are anxious to develop their proficiency in English and more willing to experiment with new methods and materials.

English as an elective subject: Japan

Japan differs from Malaysia and the Philippines in terms of the concerns raised at the beginning of this chapter. Unlike the other two countries, Japan, as a member of Kachru's 'expanding circle', does not have an institutionalized variety of English. Von Schon (1987) argues that in contexts like Japan a standard of usage should be selected which is based on a native speaker model. As she says,

> I suggest that we do NOT accept Japanese English, German English, or Russian English as legitimate dialects. These are not dialects spoken in normal everyday life, but incomplete attempts to learn American or British or some other variety. . . . For international use, we need to teach a kind of English that is comprehensible outside one's own country. (Von Schon 1987:25)

Japan also differs from Malaysia and the Philippines in that many Japanese schools support the teaching of western culture as a way of increasing student motivation. Finally, unlike Malaysia and the Philippines, Japan has never afforded English official status; the Ministry of Education does not even require English in Japanese public schools. In fact,

> English is an elective subject, one of several foreign languages approved for study at the lower secondary level. . . . In Japan most 'electives' are not choices left to the student, but are courses selected by the principal according to prefectural guidelines. Nearly all lower secondary schools follow a policy of requiring 3 years of English language instruction involving 105 class hours per year. The choice is not surprising, in part because English is one of the required subjects on university entrance examinations. (US Department of Education 1987:36)

Even though English has no official role in Japan's educational structure, its inclusion in the university entrance examination has had a profound effect on teaching in terms of student motivation, curriculum, and methodology.

Motivation

Since competency in English is tested in the national university entrance examination, many students have a high level of instrumental motivation. In fact children from elementary school upwards study English at *jukus*—private 'cram' schools that offer tutoring in various subjects. This situation is markedly different to that in Malaysia where students, because they need only take and not pass the English language examination in the fifth year of primary school, do not have a high level of instrumental motivation.

Curriculum

The curriculum in both junior and senior high schools is dictated by the Ministry of Education's Course of Study which specifies what grammar and vocabulary are to be taught and what aspects of culture, geography, history, and literature are to be dealt with. The Ministry also approves the texts that can be used in junior and senior high school English classes. The number of texts on the list is very limited; for example, presently there are only five approved texts for junior high school, with one of them, *New Horizons,* used by the majority of schools (Kitao *et al.* 1985:130).

The content of English courses, particularly at senior high school level, is heavily influenced by the university entrance examination. Reading, grammar, and translation are emphasized since these are the focus of the exam. In general, 'the purpose of the English curriculum is to train students to read and write English, relying on grammatical analysis and translation to and from Japanese as the primary methods. Instruction includes grammatical explanation, practice with basic sentence patterns, and memorization of vocabulary' (US Department of Education 1987:36).

It is ironic that, even though grammar translation is widely used as a method to prepare students for university entrance, a great many items on the test demand global skills. Christensen (1985:14–15) contends that the majority of the questions on the test 'require the application and integration of language skills: translation, listening comprehension, summaries, compositions, rephrasings and cloze.' He argues that, because of this, the best method for helping students prepare for the test is not grammar translation but a reading-centered approach: 'reading must be the main vehicle in preparing for college entrance tests' (ibid.:17). However, both the importance placed on the examination and the widespread belief among students and teachers that the grammar translation method is the best approach are contributing to the continued use of this method.

Expatriate language teachers who accept a post in a country like Japan where English is a favored foreign language and is included in a national examination can predict certain things. First, students will have a high level of instrumental motivation to learn English. Second, because there is likely to be a strictly specified curriculum designed to help students pass the national examination, teachers may find resistance among both students and administrators to any innovations in terms of both syllabus and methodology.

Conclusion

In this chapter we have explored how decisions made by Ministries of Education can affect the quality and extent of English teaching in a country. The designation of the medium of instruction, foreign language requirements, curriculum guidelines, and standards of usage all affect the

English classroom. A knowledge of the role of English in the overall curriculum will help you to make an assessment of your students' likely level of proficiency and motivation. How early students begin their study of English, how long they study it, and whether or not they must pass examinations in it, will all have an important effect on both knowledge and motivation. However, it is important to remember that the *stated* language policy of a country in terms of its designated medium of instruction, curriculum objectives, and standard of usage may not in fact be the *implemented* policy. Things like the number of required languages, the level of teacher-training, and the fluency of teachers and students will all affect what actually occurs in the classroom.

However, as we saw in the first three chapters, the educational context is not the only thing that affects language teaching. Negative attitudes toward English can arise in countries where it is seen as an obstacle to promoting a sense of nationalism. On the other hand, positive attitudes may occur in countries where English is associated with social and economic advancement. In addition, the amount of money that a country appropriates for education is likely to affect the quality and extent of English teaching. And the roles of the teacher and students in the classroom are influenced by cultural expectations. All of these contexts then—sociopolitical, economic, cultural, and educational—have an important effect on language teaching.

We turn now to an examination of one final area which affects language teaching—the institutional context. The teaching of English is affected by the day-to-day decisions of local administrators, by the quality of teachers on a staff, and by available books and equipment. Before accepting a position, you will need to assess the philosophy of the institution in which you plan to work. The background of the students and their reasons for taking English will also be important things to consider in accepting a job. Finally, it is important to make a thorough assessment of job responsibilities and job benefits before taking a position. The next chapter will discuss the importance of these institutional parameters, suggesting how they can affect language teaching.

Exploring the ideas

1 Although the Unesco recommendation cited on page 81 argues that 'the use of the mother tongue be extended to as late a stage in education as possible,' underlying this statement is the idea that there will be a transition to a language of wider communication. Therefore the statement supports a transitional model rather than a maintenance model of vernacular education. Why would those who place nationism over

nationalism support a transitional model? Why would those who support nationalism over nationism want to extend vernacular education through the tertiary level? What are the implications for vernacular languages if they are replaced by a language of wider communication such as English at tertiary level?

2 Listed below are some examples of the Minimum Learning Competencies used in the Philippines. In Nunan's (1988) terms these curriculum objectives exemplify a 'planned curriculum', i.e. they specify *what* is to be learned but not *how* it is to be learned. As a language teacher, you will need to be able to design specific classroom activities that will help students acquire the objectives outlined in the curriculum.

In order to gain experience in this skill, select one of the listed competencies and describe a specific activity that you believe would help students to acquire it. For example, one of the subskills given under 'Listening' is to 'follow a series of directions in experiments and projects.' If you select this subskill, describe a specific activity which would help students to acquire it. Be certain to use content that would be suitable for students overseas.

Minimum learning competencies
English, Grade VI (age 11 to 12)

I. Listening
A. Auditory Discrimination
1. Identify the mood of varied utterances in conversation

B. Comprehension
1. Follow a series of directions in experiments and
projects
2. Note details from informative materials
3. Give the main idea of a selection
3.1. Give titles to selection heard
4. Make inferences
5. Predict outcomes
6. Evaluate utterances, advertisements as to truth or falsity or whether they are half-truths, exaggerations or understatements

II. Speaking
1. Relay information, messages accurately using indirect discourse (request, command, statement, questions)
2. Talk about people, ideas, events
2.1. Talk about one's experiences
– Use a variety of sentences (simple, compound, complex)
– Use the correct form of verbs with nouns that are plural in form but singular in meaning

    – Use gerunds
      e.g. *Walking* is good. I enjoy *cooking.*
    – Use prepositions: *below, above, beside*
    – Use the expressions:
      too + adjective + infinitive
      hope - can, wish - could
    – Use two-word adjectives
    2.2. Talk about topics of interest
    (Source: Sibayan 1985)

3   In countries where a local variety of English exists, expatriate language teachers may have difficulty understanding their students because of the different sound patterns, grammatical structures, lexical items, and discourse patterns of the local variety. In the same way, students may have difficulty understanding the variety of English spoken by the teachers.

    If you were teaching in such a situation, how would you try to clarify those aspects of your students' language that you had problems in understanding? What would you do to help your students understand your variety of English? What strategies could you teach them to let you know when they do not understand something you said? Here you might list actual items you could teach them like 'Please could you repeat that?'

4   Malaysia and Japan offer interesting contrasts in the effects on students' motiviation of having standardized curriculum examinations. The fact that Malaysian students need only take and not pass an examination has reduced their motivation for learning English. On the other hand, in Japan, the fact that students' scores in English affect their chances of getting in to a university, makes their motiviation much higher.

    If you were teaching in a country like Malaysia, where students' motivation to learn English was not high, what would you do to try to increase it?

    If you were teaching in a country like Japan, what would you do to expand students' motivation to learn English beyond the need to pass the national examination?

Researching the ideas

1   Using the following questions as a starting point, research the role of English education in a particular country. In addition to describing the role of English teaching in the country, discuss what you think would be the effect of the stated language policies on such things as students'

motivation and proficiency level. Finally, discuss other factors in the sociopolitical, economic, cultural, and linguistic context that would either support or undermine the extent and quality of English teaching in the country, resulting perhaps in a discrepancy between stated and implemented language education policies.

a. What language(s) are used as the medium of instruction in the primary schools? In the secondary schools? In tertiary education? What language(s) are most textbooks written in at primary, secondary, and university level?

b. If English is a medium of instruction, at what point does instruction in English begin? If English is used with another language as the medium of instruction, what is the relationship between the two languages in the curriculum?

c. If English is a required subject, at what point in the educational system does the teaching of English begin? How many hours of instruction are included in the curriculum?

d. If English is one of several choices to fulfill a foreign language requirement, how popular is it?

e. What foreign language(s) other than English are taught? At what stage in education are they introduced?

f. Is there a national curriculum for English? How detailed are the learning objectives? How rigidly is the curriculum adhered to? Does the content emphasize the local culture or an anglophone culture?

g. What international or national examinations are taken by students? What is the students' attitude toward these examinations?

h. What qualifications must teachers have to teach English? Does the government sponsor in-service training programs for English teachers?

2 Much has been written on the specific phonological, morphological, syntactic, and stylistic characteristics of New Englishes.

Research the specific features of an institutionalized variety of English such as Indian English, Nigerian English, Filipino English, or Singaporean English. In your paper, include a discussion of whether or not there is support in the country for the use of the native variety of English. Do political and educational leaders or literary figures support the use of the local variety, and if so, what arguments do they offer in favor of the use of this variety? The books listed in the 'Suggestions for further reading' contain a variety of sources for this assignment.

Suggestions for further reading

Bailey, R. and **M. Gorlach** (eds.) 1982. *English as a World Language.* Ann Arbor, Mich.: The University of Michigan Press.

This book contains articles on variations in English in anglophone countries, as well as specific articles on English in the Caribbean, West Africa, East Africa, South Africa, India, Singapore, Malaysia, Hong Kong, and Papua New Guinea.

Kachru, B. (ed.) 1982. *The Other Tongue*. Oxford: Pergamon Press.
In addition to general background articles on the concept of New Englishes, the book includes specific articles on Kenyan English, Nigerian English, Indian English, Singapore English, Caribbean English, and English in Japan and China. It also has two articles on New English literatures.

Kachru, B. 1986. *The Alchemy of English*. Oxford: Pergamon Press.
This book defines the concept of institutionalized varieties of English and deals with regional norms and attitudes toward different varieties of English. It ends with a discussion of contact literatures.

Platt, J., H. Weber, and H. M. Lian. (eds.) 1984. *The New Englishes*. London: Routledge and Kegan Paul.
This book provides an excellent introduction to the topic of New Englishes. It includes an overview of their characteristics, as well as a discussion of the problems which arise from their existence.

Pride, J. (ed.) 1982. *New Englishes*. Rowley, Mass.: Newbury House Publishers.
This is a valuable reference for investigating the features of particular New Englishes. Included in the text are articles on Nigerian English, Indian English, Malaysian English, and English in Cameroon and Singapore.

Quirk, R. and H. G. Widdowson (eds.) 1985. *English in the World*. Cambridge: Cambridge University Press.
This book includes papers from an international conference entitled 'Progress in English Studies'. One quarter of the book is devoted to the issue of the English language and English literature in a global context.

Smith, L. (ed.) 1983. *Readings in English as an International Language*. Oxford: Pergamon Press.
This book contains several valuable articles on the characteristics of English as an international language and on the relationship between culture and discourse structures. Included in the collection are several articles by Smith as well as by Kachru, Strevens, and Clyne.

5 LANGUAGE TEACHING AND THE INSTITUTIONAL CONTEXT

Theoretical background

In this chapter we will explore how the institutional context of a teaching post affects various professional concerns such as classroom methodology and job responsibilities. The chapter begins with a delineation of three types of English teaching institution based on the source of funding. In this section, we examine how the funding of institutions is related to decision-making powers, extent of material resources, staff qualifications, and student population. Next, the chapter examines how institutions differ in their philosophy, in terms of their goals, preferred methodologies, and classroom policies. After examining the funding and philosophy of English teaching institutions, we focus on various professional concerns that job candidates need to consider before accepting overseas employment. The chapter ends with case studies of teaching experiences at three different kinds of institution.

English teaching institutions

Funding

In most countries, the teaching of English is a concern of both the public and private sectors: governments, foundations, and private individuals are all involved in it. The source of an institution's funding determines both the amount of resources available and who controls the funds. Who controls the funds determines, to a large extent, who is hired to teach, who is admitted to learn, and what curriculum is used. In this overview, institutions will be classified in the following way:

- *Public institutions*, i.e. those primarily supported by government funds.
- *Privately funded institutions*, i.e. those which receive the majority of their funds from external sources other than the government (for example, corporations, religious organizations).

– *Private institutions*, i.e. those which operate primarily on the funds which they themselves generate from student fees.

Public institutions

The most common type of public institution involved in the teaching of English is a primary, secondary, or post-secondary school. As was demonstrated in the discussion of Central American countries in Chapter 2, the amount of money that a government allocates to education can vary greatly. This, in turn, affects the quality and extent of English teaching. Since governments provide funds for the operation of a nation's schools, they exert, through their Ministries of Education, a great deal of control over the role of English teaching. In Chapter 4, we discussed the control Ministries of Education have over the curriculum and national examinations. In addition, they control both staff qualifications and student population.

When a government allocates only limited resources to education, the staff may not be highly qualified. As we saw, this is the case in Guatemala where only a small percentage of the teachers in the *basico* program are actually certified. On the other hand, when a government allocates generous resources to teacher training, as we saw is the case in the Philippines, the teaching skills of the staff will be constantly improving.

The student population of public institutions is largely a factor of a Ministry of Education's regulations regarding compulsory education. If public education is required of all children up to a certain age and encouraged after that, then students' ability and socio-economic background will vary greatly. On the other hand, if through tracking and national examinations, a country limits the student population, particularly at higher levels, then there will tend to be an élite student body.

If public education is not provided for all citizens of a country, or if the quality is poor, expatriate language teachers will be affected, even if they teach in private institutions. Joy (1985), whose experience was referred to in Chapter 3, points out that the greatest problems facing expatriate language teachers in Saudi Arabia are those relating to a general lack of literacy among the people. Since Saudi Arabia has a fairly high illiteracy rate, and since some students there are paid by their employers to acquire reading skills in English, expatriate language teachers often find that they are teaching a second language to students who have little or no literacy in their own language. Because of this, frequently basic reading skills have to be developed before any further language work can be done (ibid.:25). Joy's case illustrates how the teaching of English, even in private institutions, will be affected by the public education of the host country.

In some countries, Ministries attempt to involve a very broad range of citizens in education through distance education systems or what are

called 'open universities'. In Thailand, for example, Sukothai
Thammathirat Open University provides a distance education system
which allows students to study English at home through correspondence
texts and radio and television programs. The rationale for establishing this
particular university was to provide an opportunity for people to pursue a
higher education who were unable to attend a conventional type of
university due to such things as family or job commitments (Sukwiwat
1985:16). Such programs reflect a concern on the part of the country to
develop the literacy skills of its adult population.

Privately funded institutions

In privately funded institutions the resources available are related to who
provides the funds. For example, a private corporation may provide
generous funding for English teaching in order to increase the proficiency
of its staff. If the source of funding is a religious group, the extent of the
resources available will depend on the wealth of the organization and the
priority it gives to English teaching.

Who teaches and who studies in privately funded institutions is usually
solely in the hands of the funding organization. If it is a corporation, it
will specify what degrees and teaching experience are needed for employment, and the student population will likely be composed exclusively of
employees. If it is a religious group, the student population may be
composed largely of members of the particular faith, as may be the staff.
As far as the curriculum is concerned, if an institution is funded by a
corporation, a detailed curriculum in terms of both learning objectives
and content may exist to meet the on-the-job needs of the employees. On
the other hand, if an institution is funded by a religious group, while
there may be great flexibility in the English teaching objectives, religious
topics may well provide the content of the curriculum.

In some cases privately funded institutions will have greater resources
available than will publicly funded ones. For example, Anthony Tassinari,
who in 1989 was employed as an English teacher at the Arusha Catholic
Seminary in Arusha, Tanzania, wrote to me that the facilities at his school,
which is funded by the Catholic Church, were much better than at the
government-sponsored secondary schools. As he said,

> We have electricity, while other schools don't. We have books, other
> schools don't. We have a library that would be the envy of any
> secondary school in Tanzania. . . . We have a movie projector. We
> have enough paper for the students, a desk for each student, lighting
> at night, video players and plenty of videos which other schools
> don't have. (Tassinari, personal communication, April 1989)

He pointed out that the reason his school had such things is because the local administrator had contacts with individuals in the United States and Europe who could obtain equipment that was not readily available in Tanzania. In addition, even if such things had been available in the country, often the local officials could not get the foreign exchange necessary to purchase the equipment.

Private institutions

Decision-making in private institutions rests with the board of directors. This body determines staffing criteria, curriculum guidelines, and student population. Since such institutions need to generate their own funds, generally the board is interested in attracting as many students as possible to the program. In order to do this, the institution may offer a great variety of classes. For example, the American Language Center in Casablanca, in addition to a regular semi-intensive program open to all interested students, has 'tailor-made intensive or non-intensive ESP courses for bankers, doctors, students, and business people.' In addition, it offers a program for children from the ages of 4 to 14 (American Language Center of Casablanca Handbook 1988:6). The fee charged by an institution will affect the type of students who can attend it. If the fees are relatively high, the student population will be limited to people of privileged socio-economic backgrounds.

Since private institutions want to attract a large number of students, they may seek to hire highly-qualified staff so that they can point to tḥe quality of their staff in promoting their program. For example, the American Language Center in Casablanca states in their prospectus that all of the teachers have at least a bachelor's degree and most have a master's degree. In addition, some of their Moroccan teachers are professors at local universities or are English inspectors for the Ministry of Education.

The quality of private schools can vary greatly. For example, for a long time in Malaysia, they were regarded as places for dropouts from government schools. Because there is no national accreditation council for Malaysian private schools to ensure that certain minimum standards are maintained, they tended to employ teachers who had no formal English training, classes were large, and teachers were underpaid. Today, however, many of the private schools have teachers who have had a lot of professional training and they provide high quality language programs. This is largely because they are now run by educators who are trying to attract the more professionally oriented section of the population (Chitravelu 1985:15).

Implications for language teaching

An institution's source of funding can affect the language classroom in several ways. First, the source of funding determines the availability of resources. English programs operated by the governments of developed countries, by wealthy corporations, and by thriving private language schools will typically be well resourced. The source of funding also determines who has control over the curriculum. In public institutions, this control comes from a Ministry of Education. The case studies in the last chapter illustrated the role that a Ministry of Education has in shaping a nation's curriculum. In privately funded institutions, curriculum control rests with the external source of funding; very often this source has its own agenda, whether it be to increase employees' fluency in English or to promote a particular religious philosophy. If the goals of the funding source are related to on-the-job needs of employees, the curriculum will likely be one of English for Specific Purposes. Finally, because private institutions are usually controlled by a board of directors who must please their clientele, the curriculum may cater to a wide variety of needs. In all three types of institution, then, the source of funding will to a large extent determine the nature and content of the courses available.

The source of funding also affects the make-up of the staff and student population. A lack of adequate resources in any type of institution can result in an untrained staff. This means that expatriate language teachers may find themselves working alongside colleagues who have considerably less training than they do. Local teachers may either be unwilling to work closely with trained specialists for fear of appearing inadequate or, on the other hand, be eager to learn from them. Both sets of circumstances entail additional responsibilities for the expatriate teacher. As we have seen, the source of funding also plays a role in determining the make-up of the student population in terms of age, socio-economic background, and even religious belief.

Perhaps the most significant difference that an institution's source of funding has for expatriate teachers lies in the overall educational goals of public versus private institutions. Public education typically has long-term goals: for example one of its objectives is to develop literacy skills in the first language in order to teach content subjects. As was pointed out earlier, how well it handles this task will affect language teachers in private and privately funded schools. If public education does not do an adequate job in teaching literacy skills, this lack must be supplied in private schools. However, if public education has done a good job of developing literacy skills in the medium of instruction, students will then have language skills that can contribute to their success in second language learning. (For a discussion of the effect of first language learning on second language learning, see Cummins 1979, 1981.) The goals of private and privately funded institutions, on the other hand, are more modest. In general, their goals are short-term and involve more limited language objectives such as developing conversational or reading skills in English.

Philosophy

Institutions have philosophies regarding goals, methods, and policies. These may or may not be explicitly stated in an official document. Also, as was pointed out in Chapter 4, there may be a discrepancy between stated and implemented educational goals. For example, as we saw in the case of Malaysia, the Ministry of Education's stated goal of promoting communicative language teaching is not being well implemented due to inadequate teacher training and materials. While examining the stated goals of an institution does not necessarily show what it practices, it may demonstrate what it hopes to attain.

Goals

Many publicly funded institutions have a statement of goals developed by their Ministry of Education. Typically these goals reflect the function that English has in the society. For example, the Moroccan Ministry of Education specifies the following objectives of English language teaching:

> In Moroccan schools, English is taught as a foreign language. This means that the students have no opportunity to use it in their daily lives—or very rarely.
>
> But given the increasing importance for English as a language of international communication (a fact of which our students are very aware), the manifold professional and social advantages of a know-ledge of English are fairly evident. We are concerned, then, with English as a means for our learners to receive information about the world at large and to communicate their own reality to people else-where. (Ministère de l'Education Nationale 1985:5)

This statement reflects the limited role that English has in Morocco, while emphasizing its linguistic power in the international context. The document goes on to say that the immediate goal of English teaching in Morocco is to help students pass the baccalaureate examination. The longer term objectives, which stress reading skills and cultural understanding, are described as follows:

> – To train the students to achieve the capacity to have access to written materials. . . . Science students in particular, especially those undertaking research, have at one time or another to consult reference books which are available in no other language but English.
> – To get the student to adopt a tolerant attitude towards people across national barriers by giving him/her insights into the way of life of the people who speak the language. (Ministère de l'Education Nationale 1985:5)

In view of these goals, expatriate language teachers working in a Moroccan public school would quite likely find a strong emphasis on developing reading skills. Given this fact, public school students who enroll in private institutes may also be interested in developing reading skills in order to succeed in a public institution, thus illustrating another way in which private institutions can be affected by the educational goals of the public sector.

The government of Tanzania specifically links the teaching of English to larger political issues as is shown in the following statement:

> *Course Aims:* l) To give the student some basic knowledge about the English language. 2) To make the student more competent in the use of the English language so that the students can use it as a tool for self expression and international communication. 3) To develop in the students the following attitudes: (a) Commitment to the socialist development of Tanzania and to the world wide Liberation struggle. (b) Respect for African and Tanzanian culture. (Tanzanian Ministry of National Education 1982:1)

This statement suggests that the content of materials in Tanzanian public schools is likely to be political in nature with a focus on African culture.

Because private and privately funded institutions typically have linguistic rather than social goals, they generally do not emphasize a political philosophy; however, they often share with public institutions the goal of developing international communication. The Language Institute of Japan (LIOJ), for instance, in its statement of institutional philosophy specifies the following:

> The purpose of LIOJ as an institution is to encourage and foster the exchange of ideas across cultures. The success of LIOJ reflects the extent to which all who participate (faculty and staff as well as students) can develop their cross-cultural understanding and communication skills. (Language Institute of Japan 1989:1)

Methods
In some instances, in addition to stating its goals, an institution will also say how it believes learning should proceed. For example, the Asociación Cultural Hispano Norteamericana (1989) in Madrid relates its philosophy to the following learning principles:

1. The students should be the focal point of the learning process.
2. Communication is the goal of language learning.
3. Language learning is a step-by-step process.
4. Motivation is the key to students' success.
(Asociación Cultural Hispano Norteamericana 1989:1)

In attempting to promote a particular view of language learning, institutions may advocate certain methodologies. For example, the Moroccan

Ministry of Education supports a methodology which encourages learners to practice the language freely in a relaxed atmosphere. As they phrase it,

> Since English is a means of communication, the teacher should keep in mind that the students need to practise the language extensively. This practice should take place in a relaxed atmosphere in order to achieve the communicative purposes of our teaching. Anxiety and tension hamper communication. Therefore the teacher should encourage his/her students to express themselves freely. (Ministère de l'Education Nationale 1985:6)

The Tanzanian government encourages student participation through group work. It states that 'group work will be used as far as possible to develop attitudes of co-operation and self reliance' (Tanzanian Ministry of National Education 1982:1), a goal which reflects less of the pedagogic concern expressed, for example, by the Moroccan government and more of a concern with developing specific social attitudes.

Some institutions are more detailed in their statements concerning the methods they use, even naming specific methodologies. For example, the American Language Center of Casablanca (1988:6) states the following: 'Our approach in teaching all languages is eclectic. Methods and techniques used include silent way, counseling learning, total physical response, pair and small group work, cloze, and problem solving to mention a few.' Expatriate language teachers considering a position in this institution could assume that they would be allowed a good deal of leeway in the methods they use in their classes, although more traditional methodologies such as audiolingualism or grammar translation would appear, by implication, not to be encouraged.

One difficulty expatriate language teachers in private institutions may experience is that if their students are familiar with more traditional language methods because of their widespread use in public institutions, they may conclude that such methods are the proper way that languages should be taught. Thus, newer language teaching methods such as silent way or total physical response, which do not meet students' expectations about what should occur in a classroom, may not be well received. Because of this the success—or otherwise—of teachers in private institutions is likely to depend on the methods used in the larger educational context.

Policies
Institutions also have policies on such things as discipline, attendance, and grading. When an institution specifies no formal policies on these matters, this suggests that teachers will be given a good deal of discretion and responsibility. Some institutions have very clearly specified policies,

for example the American Language Center in Rabat, which states the following:

> Discipline is viewed at the Center as being the responsibility of the teachers and not, in general, of the administration. There are cases, however, where a situation gets out of control, where the recalcitrant student becomes unendurable, and/or when s/he disturbs the class to an unacceptable level. In such cases, the student should be sent to the office to be dealt with. Generally speaking, a talking to is all that is necessary to resolve problems. However, particularly with young-sters, more severe measures must be (and are) taken, such as refusing to allow the child back into class until a meeting with his/her parents has taken place. In extreme cases that have not seemed open to any other solution, the student has been temporarily, and even permanently, excluded from the Center. (American Language Center of Rabat 1990:6)

Expatriate language teachers working at the Center would then need to develop a discipline policy for their classes so that they could handle all but the most difficult discipline problems.

Harmer (1983:213) argues that all teachers should develop with their students a code of conduct in which teachers and students agree upon rules of classroom behavior. These rules might include such things as homework, attendance, and tardiness policies. The advantage of having such a code in an expatriate language teaching context is that students and teachers, coming from different cultural backgrounds, will likely have different expectations about appropriate classroom behavior. In formu-lating a code of conduct, teachers and students can discuss their differences and reach compromises. One problem some expatriate language teachers may face in developing a code is that if the students are not highly fluent in English and the teacher does not know the native language, teachers and students will not have a common language to discuss such matters. This illustrates how important it is for expatriate teachers to gain at least a working knowledge of the native language.

As far as attendance is concerned, the Center requires teachers to keep accurate information so that it can report attendance records to student sponsors. With reference to grading and exams, the Center has the following policy:

> It is important to understand that it is within the system in force at the Center, as it is in Morocco in general, for a student who feels that s/he should not have failed . . . to be given a second chance, most commonly by being allowed to re-sit the exam for the course.
>
> 1. To the above point, when a teacher believes a student really must

fail (i.e. should not re-sit the exam, nor be allowed to pass on proba-
tion), particularly when no effort was made, nor work done, nothing
done in class, etc., as complete an explanation as possible . . . ensures
that the students does, in fact, repeat and does not manage to go on
to the next level . . . (American Language Center of Rabat 1990:5)

Policies like the one stated above, in which students at the Center and
throughout Morocco are allowed to retake exams, are not found in all
countries. This highlights the fact that policies may differ cross culturally.
Because of these cross-cultural differences, expatriate teachers, even more
than local teachers, need to research carefully the goals, methods, and
policies of institutions where they are considering employment.

Implications for language teaching

The goals, methods, and policies of an institution can affect expatriate
language teachers in several ways. First, in cases such as that of Tanzania,
where the Government supports a particular political goal in its schools,
before accepting a position you would need to reflect on whether or not
you wish to support specific political views in your classroom. Second, an
institution's philosophy in terms of classroom methodology will set limits
on what are or are not considered to be acceptable classroom activities. If
you strongly support particular teaching methodologies, then it is essential
that you determine whether or not your preferences are in keeping with
the philosophy of the institution in which you hope to work.

Third, an institution may have discipline, attendance, or grading procedures that you do not find acceptable. For example, in many countries,
corporal punishment is a standard method of discipline. If you cannot
accept this method of discipline, then you should seriously consider
whether or not to accept a position in an institution which has such as
policy. In the case of attendance, if an institution, for example, has no
attendance requirements and you consider this to be important, then
again you need to weigh this factor in accepting a position. An institution's philosophy needs to be carefully investigated before accepting a
teaching position. There are, in addition, other factors of professional
concern you need to consider.

Securing employment

The major factors that you need to address before accepting a post in an
institution overseas are the following:

- First, *why* does the institution exist? What are its goals and objectives?
- Second, *who* are the people who make up the institution? Who admin-
  istrates, staffs, and attends it?

- Third, *what* is taught? What curriculum guidelines and textbooks are used?
- Fourth, *how* does learning proceed? What methods are used? What schedules are implemented?
- Fifth, *where* does the learning take place? What are the facilities like? Where, and in what size community is the institution located?

Let us consider each one of these in turn and evaluate their importance.

Goals: the why

We have already examined in some detail the goals of various institutions. As was pointed out earlier, one of the primary differences between public and private institutions lies in the extent of their commitment to their students. While state-run institutions are concerned with developing literacy skills and general knowledge, private and privately funded language schools have more limited objectives. What this suggests is that if you are working in state-run institutions, particularly in contexts where English is a medium of instruction, your task will be to develop both language and general knowledge. In addition, if you are working in this kind of context, you may be expected to promote certain political views and social attitudes. In deciding whether or not to take up a position in a public institution, therefore, you will need to consider the extent to which you support the social and political views espoused by the educational structure.

If you are working in a private or privately funded institution, on the other hand, you will more likely be expected only to develop the language skills of your students, not general knowledge nor social or political values. The exception to this could be privately funded institutions where one of the aims is to foster particular values, whether they be religious or corporate in nature.

Personnel: the who

A second area of professional concern involves the administrative, staff, and student members of the institution. Any expatriate language teacher will have certain expectations, based on their cultural background, regarding administrators' responsibilities for hiring, scheduling, and budgeting. At times these expectations may not be met. As English (1989:23) points out in her article (see pages 71–3), she was sometimes jolted by unexpected variations in class schedules or faculty meetings at her institution. She concludes that the problem rested not with the University but rather with her expectations about organization and management. In order to deal with such problems, you might employ the strategy of pragmatic ethnography discussed in Chapter 3 and investigate the role of administrators in your host country, reflecting on your own expectations regarding the role of administrators, and then applying this knowledge to determine how you might best deal with the administrative structure of the institution in which you are employed.

You will also need to consider the background of your teaching colleagues —their qualifications, nationality, and native language. As was pointed out in Chapter 4, countries vary greatly in the implementation of policies regarding staff qualifications in state-run institutions. While most countries, at least in their stated policy, require trained teachers, factors like a shortage of teachers or inadequate funds for teacher training can undermine this goal. If the staff is generally not well trained, you can expect your job to be more difficult since your students may not have a good foundation in English.

You should also investigate how many of the staff are local teachers and how many are expatriate. In some cases, private and privately funded institutions attempt to hire only native speakers since they believe students prefer this. The unfortunate aspect of this situation is that you will then have little opportunity to interact with local colleagues who could provide you with insight on the host culture and on aspects of the native language that may cause interference in learning English. A teaching staff which is composed of members of different nationalities may occasionally produce friction. Joy (1985:28), for example, describes the situation at her institution in Saudi Arabia where one-third of the staff were Americans, one-third British, and one-third Saudi Arabian. Arguments often arose about what variety of English to teach and what methods to use.

Finally, you will need to investigate who the students at the institution are. State-run institutions, if admission is not restricted in any way, may have students with a broad range of literacy skills. This means you will need to group students and individualize activities to suit their proficiency levels. In contrast, as a result of their high tuition fees, some private or privately funded institutions, may have an élite population. Also, if a private institution offers classes to meet the specific academic and professional needs of its students, the range of skills and goals of the student population will be further reduced, making it easier to meet the needs of individual students.

Curriculum: the what

The primary advantages and disadvantages of an institution having curriculum guidelines were pointed out in Chapter 4. One additional advantage to having curriculum guidelines clearly stated is that they provide a course structure and, in some cases, classroom materials. In this way they simplify the teacher's job. Expatriate language teachers who, in addition to teaching, have to adjust to a new culture, language, and housing arrangements, may initially appreciate the support of a clearly stated curriculum, particularly until they are better able to assess the needs and levels of their students. Thus, there are advantages to taking a position with an institution that has curriculum guidelines.

Methodology and scheduling: the how

How learning proceeds in an institution can be thought of in terms of two dimensions: the language teaching method and the class scheduling. As was pointed out in Chapter 4, Ministries of Education exert considerable control over classroom methodology. In the case of Japan, the decision of the Ministry to include English on the national university entrance examination has led to the widespread use of the grammar-translation method because both teachers and students believe that this method is the best preparation for this particular examination. In Tanzania, at least in its stated policy, group work and co-operation is encouraged in order to reinforce certain social values. These are only two of the ways in which teaching methods encouraged by public institutions can reflect the overall educational goals of a country.

In private institutions, however, since methods can be selected more for pedagogic reasons, primarily to develop language proficiency rather than to promote social goals, there is usually much more freedom of choice. But, as was pointed out earlier, although private institutions can often encourage a wider range of methods, students may be hesitant to use them because of their prior experience in public institutions. Hence, if you are working in a private institution, you will need to examine the methods used in the public institutions of your host country so that you are aware of any differences that exist in the choice of methodology between the two types of institution.

Class scheduling is another factor which affects the manner in which language learning occurs. Typically instruction in public institutions, with the exception of adult education programs, occurs daily over an entire school year. Private and privately funded institutions, on the other hand, often schedule classes which only meet two or three times a week for a short period of time. Because the language learning goals of short-term programs need to be limited in scope, teachers in such programs will see less progress in their students than do teachers in long-term programs. In addition, teachers in short-term programs will not have the opportunity to get to know their students as well as those in long-term programs.

As far as the time of day that classes are held is concerned, many private institutions offer classes late in the day to suit the needs of students who want to increase their English proficiency for professional on-the-job reasons or for academic reasons like passing a national examination. In such cases, because students have already completed a day of work or school, they may be quite tired. Like the length of a course, the time of day at which classes are held can have an important effect on language learning and should be taken into account by the teacher.

Student-teacher ratio is another important aspect of scheduling. Public institutions often have large classes to accommodate the needs of the general population; private institutions, however, may have smaller classes to cater to the needs of a particular population of learners. In the 'Case studies' section we will examine the experience of a teacher whose large classes required her to make changes in the kinds of activities she used. Since large classes are common in public institutions, language teachers who plan to work in state-run schools would do well to investigate activities for large classes (see question 2 in the 'Researching the ideas' section).

Facilities: the where

The final aspect of an institution that you will need to examine are its facilities, in terms of both the building itself and the resources within it. Public institutions, as a result of restricted funding, often have more limited facilities and resources than private or privately funded institutions. Poor classroom facilities, of course, are possible in any country and in any type of institution. However, while the students may be used to modest or poor physical facilities, the expatriate language teacher may take much better conditions for granted. Thus, you may find the facilities to be crowded, or cold, or stark while to the students they seem perfectly normal. If you feel uncomfortable in your surroundings, you will need to examine what aspects are particularly troublesome to you. By doing this you can determine what things you need to modify.

In some cases, for example putting up posters to brighten a dreary classroom, the changes may be easy to undertake. In other cases, however, changes may require funds or permission that are not possible to obtain. For example, if the typical classroom arrangement in your institution involves desks and chairs in straight lines, you may find resistance from both administrators and custodians to changing this. Such situations will often demand accommodations on your part that may be quite frustrating.

In institutions in many developing countries resources such as a library, duplicating machines, and audiovisual equipment are minimal or nonexistent. A lack of duplicating facilities will necessitate designing activities which do not require separate handouts. Oral directions and blackboard writing will need to be the main source of content and classroom directions. The 'Suggestions for further reading' section includes two journals that you can consult for ideas on activities which require minimal resources.

One valuable resource outside the institution itself are libraries operated by the United States Information Service and the British Council. These libraries typically contain general background reading on a variety of subjects, as well as language teaching method books and classroom textbooks. You could contact the United States Information Service and the British Council, whose addresses are given in the Appendix, to see if such facilities are available in your host country.

If it appears that few resource materials will be available in your host country, you need to plan to take more resources with you. The consequences of not taking adequate resources will be illustrated in one of the case studies. What to take will depend on the individual teaching assignment. In order to select specific texts, you can do several things. First, you should find out if the institution has a standardized curriculum. If it does, you should take measures to obtain copies of the curriculum guidelines and/or textbooks so that you can use them to determine both what background materials you will need for your own reference and what supplementary materials you may want to use in class.

If no curriculum guidelines exist, you will need to find out as much as possible about your assignment including the level of the class, the goals of the students, and the names of previous textbooks that have been used. With this information, or as much of it as you can obtain, you should do two things. First, you should carefully study a variety of publisher catalogues to see what texts are available in the skill area and at the level you are concerned with. Second, you should consult colleagues in your own country who teach classes of similar proficiency level and skill focus to see what materials they would recommend.

Whether or not curriculum guidelines exist, as was pointed out in Chapter 3, you will need to assess the cultural content of the textbooks you are considering. While a textbook may be appropriate for the proficiency level of the students, the content itself may be highly inappropriate if it is your host country's policy to focus primarily on topics relating to the local culture, and if the students lack background knowledge of anglophone cultures. Hence, while the scope and sequence of a particular textbook might be quite appropriate for an overseas teaching context, the content may need to be modified so as to be made more relevant to the local culture. Textbooks, then, should be viewed as resources that in all likelihood will need to be extensively modified to meet the local context.

Finally, you need to consider the physical location of the institution where you will be working. You will be faced with the demands of settling in a new culture and perhaps learning a new language, and it is important to establish that there is affordable housing near the institution or that convenient transportation is available to possible housing areas. Also, particularly if you can anticipate some evening classes, you will want to know about the security of the area for evening commuting.

Job responsibilities and benefits

In addition to the professional concerns described above, you of course need to clarify your own job responsibilities: for example, how many hours are you expected to teach? Are you expected to undertake curriculum planning or supervision of extracurricular activities? Are you to be involved in administering placement tests? Likewise, you need to examine the benefits of the job: for example, does it include transportation or housing? What is the salary and what currency is it paid in? Are there benefits such as health coverage, shipping of personal goods, and paid leave? As was pointed out earlier, since you are likely to have certain expectations about administrators, expectations that may not be shared by members of the host country, it is extremely important to obtain written clarification of job responsibilities and benefits.

Much of the focus of the discussion in this chapter has been on comparing public and private institutions in terms of such things as philosophy, student population, and scheduling. However, there are significant differences between private institutions alone. Private institutions can vary tremendously, and the last of the three case studies in the following section illustrates this variance.

Case studies

Public institutions: Turkey

The first case study recounts the experience of a teacher who obtained a position in a public university through a government agency. Her account illustrates two common frustrations that expatriate language teachers can face in relation to job responsibilities. First, she had to deal with a very large class size, a situation which, as was pointed out earlier, is typical of much overseas teaching, particularly in the public sector. Second, she had to cope with a lack of textbooks and duplicating facilities. The account further illustrates how frustrations which arise from such things as large classes and lack of textbooks can be compounded by two factors: first, by cross-cultural differences in expectations about how an institution should operate in terms of its administration (in this case the teacher expected to have a fixed academic calendar for planning purposes); and second, by uncomfortable living conditions. Finally, and perhaps most importantly, the account emphasizes the importance of beginning to learn the host language *before* going to the country.

The United States Council for International Exchange of Scholars frequently places Fulbright lecturers in publicly supported universities. What follows are excerpts from the final report of a Fulbright lecturer, Diane Matson Forsland, who worked at Hacettepe University in Ankara during the academic year 1987–8. The following section of the report focuses on the job responsibilities and living conditions of her post.

> As a Junior Lecturer in EFL, I was assigned four courses. Three of these (Composition, Grammar and Spoken English) were second-year classes on the intermediate-advanced level; the fourth was a third-year (advanced) class, Teaching Composition. . . .

> The classes were much too large; my smallest had 36 students and my largest had 50. This factor alone considerably increased my workload. What seemed at first like quite a light teaching assignment (8 hours per week) turned out to be more than enough to keep me busy, given a) the huge stacks of papers generated by any assignment or exam, and b) the limit on the kinds of activities which can be used for such large classes, necessitating some changes in my usual methods. . . . Another factor which (unnecessarily) increased my workload was the lack of books and xeroxing facilities. . . .

> I had almost complete freedom in planning and teaching my courses, for which I was very grateful. I prefer this type of situation because it allows for maximum creativity, which is, for me, what makes teaching fun. I was allowed to choose my own textbooks and to decide on the scope of each of my courses. Of course it was difficult to do any real planning until I had met my students and had an idea of their level. Another factor which hampered planning was the lack of any academic calendar; it was very difficult to obtain specific and consistent information about holidays, exam dates, etc. It would have been extremely helpful to have had this information in writing at the beginning of the semester. As it was, I would sometimes plan, for example, to cover a certain amount of material in a particular class on a particular day in order to prepare students for a coming exam, only to be informed (usually on very short notice) that the day in question was a holiday and that there would be no class. While I was happy to have an extra day off, knowing this at least a few weeks in advance would have been helpful. Also, I would have planned my composition courses much differently if I had known we would be without books for most of the semester. As it was we limped along, expecting them to come any day. While I enjoy inventing creative solutions to teaching problems, I also like to be well prepared and well organized; in this respect, I was quite frustrated. It was, however, a good lesson in flexibility. . . .

In general I found myself with almost no leisure time here; whatever time was left after teaching duties was taken up with household chores. Everything—shopping, cleaning, cooking, laundry, bathing —seems to take two to three times as long here. . . . In addition, there are no laundromats whatsoever, and few of the frozen convenience foods that Americans are accustomed to. The average 'supermarket' here is slightly larger than a small convenience store at home, and the average grocery store here is about the size of a hall closet. This translates into many trips to many stores—and much time. After about two months one discovers what is available and where to buy it, but at the beginning it is quite difficult—especially if one does not speak the language.

I cannot emphasize strongly enough my belief that some language training—even for a few weeks—should be provided to incoming grantees *before* they arrive. The stress of trying to cope with daily living requirements in a new culture without knowing *any* of the language could be described, at least for me, as traumatic. I have never experienced anything quite so frustrating. Even knowing only greetings and numbers would have been a tremendous help. While the Turkish people are friendly and will do everything they can to meet you halfway, this doesn't always guarantee successful communication. . . . Although I enrolled in classes here, these did not begin until several weeks after my arrival, leaving me to stumble through the most critical period—the first month—on my own. . . .

There are many other issues (such as dealing with bureaucracy) that I would like to comment on, but perhaps it's best to leave something for new grantees to discover on their own. I will just say that the key concepts in coping with just about everything here are *patience* and *flexibility.*

Privately funded institutions: Tanzania

We turn now to a case study of a privately funded institution in Tanzania. As was pointed out on page 111, the nature of privately funded institutions is largely determined by their source of funding. However, both private and privately funded institutions can be affected by public education policy in terms of such things as the success of state-run schools in developing literacy and the choice of teaching method. The following case study recounts the experience of an expatriate language teacher at a Catholic boarding school in Tanzania. Although the school curriculum includes religious instruction, the English curriculum, as we shall see, is essentially dictated by the state authorities.

The account illustrates the manner in which an institution is affected by the larger political, economic, educational, and cultural context. In this case the nature of the institution and the teacher's experience there is influenced by the country's language policies, the poor economic conditions of the country, the Tanzanian educational structure, and common Tanzanian classroom expectations. The extent of the influence of these factors highlights the importance of language teachers examining potential teaching positions not just in terms of their institutional context but also in terms of the political, economic, educational, and cultural contexts addressed in Chapters 1 to 4.

In the fall of 1988, Anthony Tassinari began teaching English at the Arusha Catholic Seminary in Tanzania, a small Catholic boarding school of ninety-five students founded in 1967 by the Catholic Church. Today in Tanzania, although English and Swahili are the co-official languages, English is used as the medium of instruction in schools. (Tanzania, as was pointed out in Chapter 1, is a Uni-modal nation which hopes to replace the use of English with Swahili, once Swahili is modernized through corpus planning.) The Tanzanian Ministry of Education, as we saw is true of many countries, has a centralized English language syllabus which specifies the content for each of the Standards (the first six years of schooling) and for each of the Forms (the grades in the lower and upper secondary schools). At the end of Form VI (grade twelve), students are required to take the National Examination. Since most of the students at the seminary plan to take this exam, the curriculum adheres to the guidelines specified by the Ministry of Education. These include a statement of what literature is to be read in Forms V and VI, much of it African literature.

The Ministry of Education provides curriculum guidelines for each level, but each school has to procure for itself the books listed in the guidelines. Textbook availability was one of several areas that proved to be extremely frustrating for Tassinari. When he arrived, he found that he was unable to buy any of the listed books since the government printing press was not printing textbooks at that time. As a result, he had to drive 170 miles to Kenya in order to buy books for his students. This demonstrates the manner in which the economic conditions of a country can affect the language classroom in very real ways.

Tassinari had no administrative constraints on his choice of methodology. However, he soon found that his students had common culturally influenced expectations about what should occur in a classroom. In this case, the students expected the teacher to concentrate on explaining the grammar points which would be included on the National Examination. In general, the students wanted to be told only what they would need to know in English to pass the examination, a desire which, as we have seen, is shared by students in several other countries.

Tassinari's responsibilities at the school consisted of teaching sixteen periods a week (forty minutes per period) with an average class size of eight students. As an expatriate teacher, his teaching load and class size were lighter than those of most of the Tanzanian teachers. In addition to his teaching responsibilities, he supervised all the duties of the teachers' house and kitchen, moderated the English debate club, and managed some of the farming projects. (According to official government policy, all schools in Tanzania are supposed to raise their own food as part of the country's growth toward independence and self-reliance, so the seminary had its own farm.)

As was pointed out on page 111, the facilities at the seminary were much better than those in other Tanzanian schools: it had desks, electricity (but operating only from 7 p.m. to 10 p.m. each day), a library, and a movie projector. However, since throughout Tanzania paper is quite expensive, Tassinari had to limit his use of paper and ask students to always use both sides of every sheet, an example of how available resources affect the choice of language activities.

Tassinari's advice to anyone planning to teach overseas is to find out 'what you are going to be teaching, what reference materials are available and who you will be teaching,' advice which, as was pointed out earlier, all expatriate teachers would be wise to act upon. Tassinari had not realized that there would be such an emphasis on African literature. Because of this, he brought no African literary texts with him. However, he did anticipate that school supplies would not be readily available and so he brought with him a stock of paper, pens, pencils, erasers, staples, and pencil sharpeners—all of which proved to be quite valuable. As is evident from Tassinari's experience, investigating the professional dimensions of a job before going overseas is even more critical in developing countries than in developed countries since it is often quite difficult to get things that developed countries take for granted such as textbooks and school supplies.

Private institutions: Spain and Japan

In this case study two private institutions are compared, the Language Institute of Japan (LIOJ) and the Asociación Cultural Hispano Norteamericana (ACHNA), both located in industrialized countries yet differing significantly in their philosophy, student population, scheduling, and teaching responsibilities and benefits. After describing the differences in the institutions, the case study ends with a discussion of the advantages that each institution offers for language teachers. In the 'Exploring the ideas' section at the end of the chapter language teachers are asked to consider which of these institutions they would prefer to be employed by, and why.

ACHNA has two centers, one in Madrid and the other in Badajoz, with a total of over 100 teachers and as many as 4,800 students enrolled in the program. Most of the students are adults, many of whom are university students and professionals. The majority of students attend the non-intensive program which typically consists of twenty-five hours of instruction, one hour a day for five weeks. In order to provide hours that are convenient for a wide range of needs, classes meet from 8a.m. to 10p.m.

In order to attract as many students as possible, ACHNA, like other private institutions, also offers several special classes such as English for Executives, Preparation for the TOEFL, and children's classes. Most classes have around eighteen students. Teachers are expected to adhere to a fixed curriculum, although they may decide how to use the textbooks and may supplement them (ACHNA 1989).

LIOJ, located in Odawara, a small city south of Tokyo, provides a four-week intensive Residential Business Communication Program. Most of the students are professionals from top companies and they attend class five days a week from 8a.m. to 8p.m. with a lunch and supper break. Class size is small, with six to eight students. According to LIOJ, this small class size allows teachers to get to know their students quite well. In fact, teachers are encouraged to spend a good deal of time with their students outside of class at coffee shops, downtown, and in their homes.

LIOJ, like ACHNA and other private institutes, does offer other special Community Programs which are non-intensive and cater to a wide range of ages and needs. All teachers in the Residential Program also teach in the Community Program (LIOJ 1989). Teachers are given a great deal of latitude in designing their own materials; according to LIOJ (1989:1), a number of ESL texts have been published by faculty members. The choice of textbook is up to the teachers, and they are encouraged to be facilitators rather than lecturers and to get students involved in problem-solving activities.

The responsibilities of the teaching staff at the two institutions differ as might be expected given the contrasting nature of the two programs. At ACHNA, teachers are expected to teach twenty hours per week, help with registration, and attend occasional workshops. If teachers so wish, they can take additional employment outside the center such as tutoring or consulting. The responsibilities of teachers at LIOJ are more demanding. Teachers may be scheduled to work up to thirty periods a week: this includes teaching, administrative and residential responsibilities such as class outings, and student evaluations. In addition to their teaching, they must eat at least seven meals a week with the students and attend cocktail parties and other evening programs. These responsibilities are in keeping with the residential nature of the program. As the Institute states in its materials,

> The single most important aspect of LIOJ is the residential nature of the Business Program. Though classroom work is important, we at LIOJ feel strongly that the personal contact we have with our students is the single most important factor in giving both the faculty and the students an experience that goes beyond linguistic parameters. (LIOJ 1989:3)

Perhaps in order to be sure that they have time to develop this personal contact with their students, teachers at LIOJ are not allowed to work outside of the Institute.

In keeping with the differences in job responsibilities, the benefits of the two institutions differ. At ACHNA teachers have a nine-month to one-year contract and receive their salary in pesetas. No bonuses are included, or housing benefits, although teachers do get medical insurance, Spanish social security retirement benefits, and a one-month paid vacation in the summer.

At LIOJ teachers have a one-year contract and are paid in yen; they receive a bonus for each one-year contract they complete. They also get seven weeks of paid vacation. There are several incentives for teachers to complete and to extend their contracts. First, the annual bonus increases each year as does the salary. Second, teachers who stay more than one year are entitled to national health insurance and a retirement bonus to be paid at the completion of their final contract. Teachers also get housing support which helps to cover initial agent's fees and gift money when moving into an apartment. However, this support is paid only when the teacher leaves LIOJ upon successful completion of their final contract. If teachers break their contracts, they are not awarded their benefits.

Expatriate language teachers who were considering these two jobs would need to weigh several factors. Obviously one of the first considerations would be their location; not only the contrasting countries and cultures, but the size of the cities in which the institutes are situated. Beyond these very important considerations, however, would be several professional concerns. One of the primary differences between the two institutions involves their scheduling. While ACHNA has a non-intensive program typical of many private institutions, LIOJ, less typically, has an intensive residential program. Because of this difference in scheduling, ACHNA is, in many ways, a less demanding job in terms of the amount of time teachers are expected to hold class and be with their students.

However, while more demanding, LIOJ offers some professional advantages. The residential nature of the program, along with the small class size, would allow teachers to get to know their students much better and to see more progress in their language development. In considering these jobs expatriate teachers would need to decide whether or not they would be willing to make the additional professional time commitment to attain these benefits. LIOJ and ACHNA also differ in their curriculum, with ACHNA providing a fixed curriculum and LIOJ giving teachers great latitude in their choice of textbooks. As was pointed out on page 120, having curriculum guidelines can make the initial adjustment to a new job and culture easier, a factor which would also make ACHNA a less demanding job.

Another thing to consider is how long one plans to stay in a country. LIOJ provides several incentives for teachers to stay more than one year. Finally, teachers would need to examine how much variety they would like in their professional experience. At ACHNA teachers are allowed to do outside work which permits them to undertake tutoring and consulting, something they are not allowed to do at LIOJ. Many factors then, relating to responsibilities and benefits, need to be carefully weighed, factors which involve both an individual's teaching philosophy, as well as their personal preferences regarding the length and intensity of a teaching post.

Conclusion

In this chapter we have examined how an institution's source of funding determines the amount of resources available, as well as who makes important hiring, admittance, and curriculum decisions. The philosophy of an institution includes its goals, methods, and procedural policies. In considering whether or not to take up a teaching position, it is important for teachers to ascertain if they can accept and support the philosophy of the institution in which they may be working. In addition, they need to investigate the qualifications of the institution's staff, its student population, curriculum, methodology, facilities, and class schedule, as well as the responsibilities and benefits of the job.

The experience of the Fulbright scholar in Turkey demonstrates how teaching is only one part of an international experience. The living conditions, language, people, and culture all add to the richness—and potential frustrations—of the experience. The way in which an institution is affected by the larger context in which it operates is highlighted by the second case study on the Catholic seminary in Tanzania. The case study on LIOJ and ACHNA exemplifies the manner in which institutions vary widely in their purpose and staff responsibilities. Because of this kind of variation, job candidates need to carefully investigate and compare different teaching positions before accepting a post. Each context that we have examined in this book—the sociopolitical, economic, cultural, educational, and institutional—all interact with one another to define the precise nature of a teaching position.

While it is extremely important to do as much preparation and reading as possible before going abroad, there will still be elements for which you are not prepared, elements that can lead to cross-cultural misunderstandings and frustration. When such frustrations arise, perhaps the best thing to keep in mind is that as guests in a country, it is not the responsibility of expatriate teachers to change the host culture, nor the way that English is taught there; rather their role is to teach the language as best they can within the parameters of their teaching position, parameters which have been defined by the different contexts we have explored in this book. Above all, it is important to remember that as an expatriate teacher, in the end, although there will be frustrations, you stand to gain a global perspective that will enrich the rest of your life.

Exploring the ideas

1 The chapter contains examples of various statements of institutional philosophy regarding goals and methods, some dealing with the importance of knowing English for international communication and cross-cultural understanding, some relating English instruction to political goals, and still others advocating specific methodologies.

What goals and methodology would you like to see supported by the institution where you work? If an institution advocates goals and methods that you do not support, would you still consider accepting a teaching position there? Are there other factors about an institution such as its curriculum, student population, or scheduling that would lead you to accept a position in spite of the fact that the institution had goals and methods that you do not favor? What are these other factors?

2 As we saw in the chapter, some institutions, when stating their philosophy, specify a particular stance on student discipline. In discussing the issue of student discipline, Harmer (1983:210–12) contends that ideally an institution should have a recognized system for dealing with problem classes and students since 'ultimately a student who causes a severe problem has to be handled by the school authority rather than by the teacher on his own and it is therefore in the teachers' interest to see that there is a coherent policy.'

What kind of discipline policy would you like the institution where you are employed to have? What kinds of behavior do you think constitute discipline problems, and how should such problems be handled?

If you were teaching in an institution which had no policy, what strategies would you use in your own classroom to handle discipline problems? Harmer maintains that each class should establish a code of conduct so that students know the rules of behavior of the class. What things do you believe would be important to include in such a code?

3 The case study on LIOJ and ACHNA presents an overview of the responsibilities and benefits of teaching positions in two contrasting private institutions.

If you were offered teaching positions at both of these institutions, which would you accept and why? Would you be willing to make the additional professional commitments demanded by LIOJ? If so, why? What other factors regarding job responsibilities and benefits would lead you to make your decision?

4 Tassinari, in his teaching experience in Tanzania, faced two problems regarding classroom materials: first, the classroom texts were quite difficult to obtain; and second, he found he did not have with him the teaching reference materials on African literature that he would have found very useful. Forsland, in her account, indicates that she had to do without textbooks for most of the semester.

If you were faced with a similar situation in which the required classroom textbooks were difficult or impossible to obtain, what would you do? If you were in a position where you did not have the reference materials you needed, what steps would you take to obtain these? Here you might consider both resources you could get within the host country, as well as those you could obtain from overseas.

5 Forsland's frustrations with her teaching responsibilities were compounded by the difficult living conditions. These problems made it less easy than it might have been for her to adjust to the job and the country. Kohls (1984:52) notes additional factors which can impede an individual's adjustment to living in a foreign culture such as lack of mobility because of a country's political restrictions on movement, a slow pace of life, and social indirectness.

List other factors which you believe may contribute to adjustment problems in living overseas. Then discuss what strategies you might employ to deal with these problems.

Researching the ideas

1 Dealing with discipline problems is part of classroom management. Often effective classroom management strategies can help to avoid discipline problems from arising in the first place. These strategies include such things as developing a positive class atmosphere, making the classroom attractive, and knowing the students' background and interests.

Research good classroom management strategies including such things as ways to utilize students' interest to develop materials, ways to vary classroom organization from teacher-centered to student-centered, and ways to enhance a classroom's appearance. Describe some of these and, in your paper, be certain to include a discussion of how you think the classroom management strategies you have chosen would need to be adjusted by expatriate language teachers in order to deal with cross-cultural differences. The following are two sources you might begin with:

Harmer, J. 1983. *The Practice of English Language Teaching*. New York: Longman.

Underwood, M. 1987. *Effective Class Management*. New York: Longman.

2 Forsland's experience of being faced with large classes is typical of the teaching situation in many countries, particularly in public institutions.

Research various strategies for dealing with large classes. Include specific activities for speaking, reading, listening, and writing that can be used with large classes and indicate how they might require adaptation for particular cultural contexts. One resource you might begin with is the following:

Nolasco, R. and L. Arthur. 1988. *Large Classes*. London: Macmillan.

In addition, you might consult the journals and teacher reference series listed in the 'Suggestions for further reading'.

Suggestions for further reading

The following journals frequently contain articles on teaching English overseas and provide valuable information on specific institutions and countries. In addition, both journals include articles on strategies for dealing with the large classes and limited resources that often exist in developing countries.

English Teaching Forum is written specifically for teachers of English outside the United States and distributed abroad by American Embassies. In the United States subscriptions are available from the Superintendent of Documents, US Government Printing Office, Washington, DC 20402.

ELT Journal is concerned with teaching English both in ESL and in EFL contexts; thus, it has fewer articles applicable to overseas teaching than *English Teaching Forum*. However, it does have practical articles describing teaching activities that can be used in non-anglophone countries. Subscriptions are available from the Journal Subscriptions Department, Oxford University Press, Pinkhill House, Southfield Road, Eynsham, Oxford OX8 1JJ.

An excellent resource for general background reading on individual countries is:

Kohls, R.L. and **V. L. Tyler.** 1988. *Area Studies Resources.* Utah: Brigham Young University Press. (Available from Brigham Young University, Publication Services, 280 HRCH, Provo, Utah 84602.)

This contains information on books, databases, films, videos, and maps dealing with specific countries. Of particular interest for researching individual countries are 'Country Profiles', books which contain detailed geographic, historic, social, and political information in specific countries.

GLOSSARY

code-switching: Shifting from the use of one language to another within a conversation. The use of code-switching presupposes an individual who is highly fluent in more than one language.

corpus planning: Decisions made regarding the development of a language so that it can be used for more functions in a society. It includes such things as developing the vocabulary of a language or determining its standard of usage.

creole: A language which develops from a *pidgin* when used by a community as a native language. Creoles have more lexical terms and more grammatical distinctions than pidgins and are used for more functions in a society.

diglossia: A situation in which two varieties of a language are used within a society, each with particular functions. Often one variety is the High variety which is used in formal domains like the government, and the other the Low variety is used in intimate domains like the family.

English as an auxiliary language (EAL): A situation in which English is used as one of several languages by residents of a country to communicate among themselves. Thus, English is used as an *intranational language.* The use of English in the Philippines or India exemplifies this situation.

English as a language of wider communication (ELWC): A situation in which non-native speakers use English primarily to communicate with residents of another country. Thus, English is used primarily as an *international language.* The use of English by Japanese or Germans with individuals from another country exemplifies this situation.

English as a second language (ESL): A situation in which non-native speakers resident in an English-speaking country use English outside their immediate family or ethnic community. Non-native speakers of English who reside in the United States or Great Britain exemplify this situation.

English for specific purposes: A branch of English teaching designed to help students attain specific occupational and/or professional goals. Particular types of ESP courses include the following: English for academic purposes (EAP); English for science and technology (EST), and English for occupational purposes (EOP).

indigenous language: A language spoken by the original inhabitants of a country. Xhosa in South Africa or Navajo in the United States exemplify such languages.

interlanguage: The variety of a language spoken by language learners before they develop full competence in it.

language spread: An increase in the use of a language or language variety which is frequently the result of language planning decisions. In order to increase the use of a particular language, a country can do such things as designate it as an official language or standardize its writing system.

lingua franca: A language used habitually by people who have different first languages in order to communicate for certain specific purposes. English can be used as a lingua franca both within countries like India and between individuals from different countries.

mother tongue: The language one acquires as a child and uses within the family.

nationalism: The attachment of a people to such things as their culture, religion, history, and language. When such feelings are widely held, there is support for those language decisions that promote a sense of national identity.

nationism: The concern of a people for the efficient workings of the government. When such concern is widespread, there is support for those language decisions that best serve the political and economic interests of the country.

nativized English (also referred to as *institutionalized English* or *New English*): A variety of English which arises when English is used as one of several languages of communication within a country (see *English as an auxiliary language*) and speakers have little contact with people from countries where English is the first language. Typically in such a context unique phonological, morphological, lexical, syntactic, and stylistic features develop. The English spoken in countries like Nigeria, India, and the Philippines exemplify nativized varieties.

official language: A language which a government uses to conduct some of its official business. Generally, the country recognizes the special status of the language in one of its government documents and promotes its use in some way.

pidgin: A simplified language which has no native speakers and is used as a *lingua franca*, often for trade purposes. It typically develops in language contact situations where one or more language groups come in contact; often one group has more political dominance than the others.

status planning: Decisions made regarding the role of various languages within a country. It includes such decisions as which languages will have official status in the government and which language will be used as the medium of instruction in schools.

teaching English to speakers of other languages (TESOL): A term used to refer to the teaching of English as a second, foreign, or additional language. The same term is used to refer to the international professional organization of English teachers.

vernacular language: The first language of a group socially or politically dominated by another group with a different language. Basque in Spain or Spanish in the United States exemplify such languages.

BIBLIOGRAPHY

Abbott, G. 1984. 'Should we start digging new holes?' *ELT Journal* 38:2, 98–102.

Adaskou, K., D. Britten, and **B. Fahsi.** 1989. 'Cultural content of a secondary English course for Morocco.' *ELT Journal* 44:1, 3–10.

Alptekin, C. and **M. Alptekin.** 1984. 'The question of culture.' *ELT Journal* 38:1, 14–20.

American Language Center of Casablanca. 1988. *Handbook for Personnel.* Casablanca: American Language Center.

American Language Center of Rabat. 1990. *Policies and Procedures for Teachers.* Rabat: American Language Center.

Asociación Cultural Hispano Norteamericana. 1989. *ACHNA's Philosophy for English Teaching.* Madrid: Asociación Cultural Hispano Norteamericana.

Augustin, J. 1982. 'Regional standards of English in peninsular Malaysia' in J. Pride (ed.): *New Englishes.* Rowley, Mass.: Newbury House Publishers.

Bailey, R. and **M. Gorlach** (eds.) 1982. *English as a World Language.* Ann Arbor, Mich.: The University of Michigan Press.

Balhorn, M. and **J. Schneider.** 1987. 'Challenges of teaching EFL in Korean universities.' *TESOL Newsletter* 21:5, 15.

Bautista, M.L. 1988. 'Domains of English in the 21st Century' in A. Gonzalez (ed.): *The Role of English and Its Maintenance in the Philippines.* Manila: Solidaridad Publishing House.

Bickerton, D. 1975. *Dynamics of a Creole System.* Cambridge: Cambridge University Press.

Bowers, J. 1968. 'Language Problems and Literacy' in J. Fishman, C. Ferguson, and J. Das Gupta (eds.): *Language Problems of Developing Nations.* New York: John Wiley and Sons.

Boyd, J.R. and **M.A. Boyd.** 1986. *Beginning Listening Cycles.* Normal, Ill.: Abaca Books.

British Council. 1979. *English Teaching Profile: Lesotho.* ERIC Document, No. ED 234 605.

British Council. 1981. *English Teaching Profile: Burma.* ERIC Document, No. ED 234 605.

British Council. 1982. *English Teaching Profile: Peru.* ERIC Document, No. ED 231 196.

Brown, H.D. 1986. 'Learning a second culture' in J. Valdes (ed.): *Culture Bound.* Cambridge: Cambridge University Press.

Brown, H.D. 1987. *Principles of Language Learning and Teaching.* Englewood Cliffs, NJ: Prentice-Hall.

Burnaby, B. and **Y. Sun.** 1989. 'Chinese teachers' views of western language teaching: Context informs paradigms.' *TESOL Quarterly* 23:2, 219–38.

Chitravelu, N. 1985. *The Status and Role of English in Malaysia.* A research report prepared for the United States Information Agency.

Christensen, T. 1985. *University Entrance Examinations and English Teaching in Japan—A Non-Japanese Evaluation.* ERIC Document, No. ED 281 352.

Conrad, A. and **J. Fishman.** 1977. 'English as a World Language: The Evidence' in J. Fishman *et al.* (eds.): *The Spread of English.* Rowley, Mass.: Newbury House Publishers.

Cooper, R.L. (ed.) 1982. *A Framework for the Study of Language Spread.* Arlington, Va.: Center for Applied Linguistics.

Cooper, R.L. 1983. 'Language planning, language spread and language change' in C. Kennedy (ed.): *Language Planning and Language Education.* London: George Allen and Unwin.

Cooper, R.L. 1989. *Language Planning and Social Change.* Cambridge: Cambridge University Press.

Cooper, R.L. and **F. Seckbach.** 1977. 'Economic incentives for the learning of a language of wider communication: A case study' in J. Fishman *et al.* (eds.): *The Spread of English.* Rowley, Mass.: Newbury House Publishers.

Crandall, J., P. Miller, C. Spohnholz, and **A. Wederspahn.** 1985. *English Language Assessment in Central America.* ERIC Document, No. ED 275 176.

Cummins, J. 1979. 'Linguistic interdependence and the educational development of bilingual children.' *Review of Educational Research* 49:2, 222–51.

Cummins, J. 1981. 'The role of primary language development in promoting educational success for language minority students in California State Department of Education' in *Schooling and Language Minority Students: A Theoretical Framework*. Los Angeles, Calif.: Evaluation, Dissemination, and Assessment Center, California State University, Los Angeles.

Damen, L. 1987. *Culture Learning: The Fifth Dimension in the Language Classroom*. Reading, Mass.: Addison-Wesley Publishing.

Davies, A. 1989. 'Is International English an Interlanguage?' *TESOL Quarterly* 23:3, 447–69.

DeFilippo, J. and **C. Skidmore.** 1984. *Skill Sharpeners*, Level 1. Reading, Mass.: Addison-Wesley Publishing.

Eastman, C. 1983. *Language Planning: An Introduction*. San Francisco, Calif.: Chandler and Sharp Publishers.

Enga, H.L. 1982. *Ways: Socio-cultural Aspects of TESL in Japan*. Unpublished Master's thesis, School for International Training, Brattleboro, Vermont.

English, S. 1989. 'Teacher shock in Francophone Africa.' *TESOL Newsletter* 23:1,23.

Fasold, R. 1984. *The Sociolinguistics of Society*. New York: Basil Blackwell.

Ferguson, C. 1959. 'Diglossia.' *Word* 15,325–40.

Ferguson, C. 1968. 'Language development' in J. Fishman, C. Ferguson, and J. Das Gupta (eds.): *Language Problems of Developing Nations*. New York: John Wiley and Sons.

Fishman, J. 1968. 'Nationality-nationalism and nation-nationalism' in J. Fishman, C. Ferguson, and J. Das Gupta (eds.): *Language Problems of Developing Nations*. New York: John Wiley and Sons.

Fishman, J. 1969. 'National languages and languages of wider communication in developing nations.' *Anthropological Linguistics* 11,111–35.

Fishman, J. 1972. *Sociolinguistics: A Brief Introduction*. Rowley, Mass.: Newbury House Publishers.

Fishman, J. (ed.) 1974. *Advances in Language Planning*. The Hague: Mouton.

Fishman, J. 1977a. 'The spread of English as a new perspective for the study of "language maintenance and language shift" ' in J. Fishman *et al.* (eds.): *The Spread of English*. Rowley, Mass.: Newbury House Publishers.

Fishman, J. 1977b. 'Knowing, using and liking English as an additional language' in J. Fishman *et al.* (eds.): *The Spread of English*. Rowley, Mass.: Newbury House Publishers.

Fishman, J., R. Cooper, and **A. Conrad** (eds.) 1977. *The Spread of English*. Rowley, Mass.: Newbury House.

Fishman, J. 1982. 'Sociology of English as an additional language' in B.B. Kachru (ed.): *The Other Tongue*. New York: Pergamon Press.

Galang, R. 1988. 'The language situation of Filipino Americans' in S.L. McKay and S.L. Wong (eds.): *Language Diversity: Problem or Resource?* New York: Newbury House Publishers.

Gardner, R. and **W. Lambert.** 1972. *Attitudes and Motivation in Second Language Learning*. Rowley, Mass.: Newbury House Publishers.

Goldman, S. and **R. McDermott.** 1987. 'The culture of competition in American schools' in G. Spindler (ed.): *Education and Cultural Process: Anthropological Approaches*. Prospect Heights, Ill.: Ablex Publishing Corporation.

Gonzalez, A. 1982. 'English in the Philippines mass media' in J. Pride (ed.): *New Englishes*. Rowley, Mass.: Newbury House Publishers.

Gonzalez, A. 1988a. 'The Dilemma of English' in A. Gonzalez (ed.): *The Role of English and Its Maintenance in the Philippines*. Manila: Solidaridad Publishing House.

Gonzalez, A. 1988b. 'English and economics in the Philippines' in A. Gonzalez (ed.): *The Role of English and Its Maintenance in the Philippines*. Manila: Solidaridad Publishing House.

Harmer, J. 1983. *The Practice of English Language Teaching*. New York: Longman.

Hartshone, K.B. 1987. 'Language policy in African education in South Africa, 1910–1985, with particular reference to the issue of medium of instruction' in D. Young (ed.): *Bridging the Gap*. Cape Town: Maskew Miller Longman.

Harvey, P. 1985. 'A lesson to be learned: Chinese approaches to language learning.' *ELT Journal* 39,183–6.

Heath, S.B. 1984. 'Linguistics and education.' *Annual Review of Anthropology* 13, 251–74.

Hill, G. 1982. 'English in Brunei: Second language or foreign language?' *World Language English* 1, 24-42.

Hurst, C. 1989. 'How to obtain international employment in ESL, K–12.' *TESOL Newsletter* 12, 3-4.

Hutchinson, T. and **A. Waters.** 1987. *English for Specific Purposes.* Cambridge: Cambridge University Press.

Jernudd, B. and **J. Das Gupta.** 1971. 'Towards a theory of language planning' in J. Rubin and B. Jernudd (eds.): *Can Language be Planned?* Honolulu, HI: The University Press of Hawaii.

Jibril, M. 1982. 'Nigerian English: An introduction' in J. Pride (ed.): *New Englishes.* Rowley, Mass.: Newbury House Publishers.

Joy, C. 1985. *Guidelines for Prospective EFL Teachers in Saudi Arabia.* Unpublished Master's Thesis, School for International Training, Brattleboro, Vermont.

Judd, E. 1987. 'Teaching English to speakers of other languages: A political act and a moral question.' *TESOL Newsletter* 21:1, 15–16.

Kachru, B. 1982. 'Models for non-native Englishes' in B. Kachru (ed.): *The Other Tongue.* Oxford: Pergamon Press.

Kachru, B. 1989. 'Teaching World Englishes.' *Indian Journal of Applied Linguistics* 15:1, 85-95.

Kachru. B. 1986. *The Alchemy of English.* Oxford: Pergamon Press.

Kennedy, C. (ed.) 1983. *Language Planning and Language Education.* London: George Allen and Unwin.

Kitao, K., S.K. Kitao, K. Nozawa, and **M. Yamamoto.** 1985. 'Teaching English in Japan' in Kitao, K. (ed.): *TEFL in Japan: JALT 10th Anniversary Collected Papers.* Tokyo: JALT.

Kohls, R.L. 1984. *Survival Kit for Overseas Living.* Yarmouth, Me.: Intercultural Press.

Kohls, R.L. and **V.L. Tyler.** 1988. *Area Studies Resources.* Utah: Brigham Young University Press.

Kramsch, C. 1987. 'Socialization and literacy in a foreign language: Learning through interaction.' *Theory into Practice* 26:4, 243–50.

Lambert. W. 1972. *Language, Psychology and Culture: Essays by Wallace E. Lambert.* Stanford, Calif.: Stanford University Press.

Language Institute of Japan. 1989. *General Information 1989.* Odawara, Japan: Language Institute of Japan.

Lowenberg, P. 1986a. 'Non-native varieties of English: nativization, norms, and implications.' *Studies in Second Language Acquisition* 8:1, 1-18.

Lowenberg, P. 1986b. 'Sociolinguistic context and second-language acquisition: acculturation and creativity in Malaysian English.' *World Englishes* 5:1, 71-83.

Lowenberg, P. 1989. 'Testing English as a world language: Issues in assessing non-native proficiency' in J. Alatis (ed.): *Language Teaching, Testing and Technology: Lessons from the Past with a View Toward the Future.* Washington, DC: Georgetown University Press.

Lukmani, Y. 1972. 'Motivation to learn and language proficiency.' *Language Learning* 22, 261–74.

Maley, A. 1986. 'XANADU—"A miracle of rare device": The teaching of English in China' in J. Valdes (ed.): *Culture Bound.* Cambridge: Cambridge University Press.

Meerkotter, D. 1987. 'The struggle for liberation and the position of English in South Africa' in D. Young (ed.): *Language Planning and Medium in Education.* Cape Town: The Language Education Unit of the University of Cape Town.

Mehan, H. 1981. 'Ethnography of bilingual education' in H. Trueba, G. Guthrie, and K. Au (eds.): *Culture and the Bilingual Classroom.* Rowley, Mass.: Newbury House Publishers.

Ministère de l'Education Nationale. 1985. *Anglais.* Rabat: Ministère de l'Education Nationale.

Mohatt, G. and **F. Erickson.** 1981. 'Cultural differences in teaching styles in an Odawa school: A sociolinguistic approach' in H. Trueba, G. Guthrie, and K. Au (eds.): *Culture and the Bilingual Classroom.* Rowley, Mass.: Newbury House Publishers.

Munby, J. 1978. *Communicative Syllabus Design.* Cambridge: Cambridge University Press.

Ndebele, N. 1986. 'The English language and social change in South Africa.' Keynote lecture delivered at the Jubilee Conference of the English Academy of South Africa, September, l986.

Noss, R. 1986. *The Status and Role of English Language in ASEAN Countries: A Regional Assessment.* A research report prepared for the United States Information Agency.

Nunan, D. 1988. *The Learner Centred Curriculum.* Cambridge: Cambridge University Press.

Osterloh, K. 1986. 'Intercultural differences and communicative approaches to foreign-language teaching in the Third World' in J. Valdes (ed.): *Culture Bound.* Cambridge: Cambridge University Press.

Otanes, F.T. 1988. 'The state of English language teaching in the educational system today' in A. Gonzalez (ed.): *The Role of English and Its Maintenance in the Philippines.* Manila: Solidaridad Publishing House.

Parker, O. *et al.* 1986. 'Cultural clues to the Middle Eastern student' in J. Valdes (ed.): *Culture Bound.* Cambridge: Cambridge University Press.

Pascasio, E. 1988. 'The present role and domains of English in the Philippines' in A. Gonzalez (ed.): *The Role of English and Its Maintenance in the Philippines.* Manila: Solidaridad Publishing House.

Paulston, C.B. 1983. 'Language planning' in C. Kennedy, (ed.): *Language Planning and Language Education.* London: George Allen and Unwin.

Pike, K. 1954. *Language in Relation to a Unified Theory of the Structure of Human Behavior.* Vol. 1. Glendale, Calif.: Summer Institute of Linguistics.

Platt, J., H. Weber, and **H.M. Lian.** 1984. *The New Englishes.* London: Routledge and Kegan Paul.

Prator, C. 1968. 'The British heresy in TESL' in J. Fishman, C. Ferguson, and J. Das Gupta (eds.): *Language Problems of Developing Nations.* New York: John Wiley and Sons.

Pride, J. (ed.) 1982. *New Englishes.* Rowley, Mass.: Newbury House Publishers.

Prucha, J. 1985. *Foreign Language Needs: Theory and Empirical Evidence in Czechoslovakia.* ERIC Document, No. ED 266 637.

Quirk, R. and **H.G. Widdowson** (eds.) 1985. *English in the World.* Cambridge: Cambrdge University Press.

Rubin, J. 1983. 'Bilingual education and language planning' in C. Kennedy (ed.): *Language Planning and Language Education.* London: George Allen and Unwin.

Rubin, J. and **B.H. Jernudd** (eds.) 1971. Can Language be Planned? Honolulu, HI: The University Press of Hawaii.

Rubin, J., B.H. Jernudd, J. Das Gupta, J. Fishman, and **C. Ferguson** (eds.) 1977. *Language Planning Processes.* The Hague: Mouton.

Salhi, R. 1984. 'Language Planning: A Case Study of English in Tunisia.' Unpublished Ph.D. dissertation, Faculty of Letters, University of Tunis.

Santiago, I. 1982. 'Third world vernacular/bi-multilingual curricula issues' in B. Hartford *et al.* (eds.): *Issues in International Bilingual Education.* New York: Plenum Press.

Sato, C. 1982. 'Ethnic styles in classroom discourse' in M. Hines and W. Rutherford (eds.): *On TESOL '81*. Washington, DC: TESOL.

Shaw, W. 1983. 'Asian student attitudes toward English' in L. Smith (ed.): *Readings in English as an International Language*. Oxford: Pergamon Press.

Sibayan, B. 1985. *The Status and Role of English and Pilipino in the Philippines*. A research report prepared for the United States Information Agency.

Smith, L. 1983. 'Some Distinctive Features of EIL vs. ESOL in English Language Education' in L. Smith (ed.): *Readings in English as an International Language*. Oxford: Pergamon Press.

Smith, L. 1985. 'EIL versus ESL/EFL: What's the difference and what difference does the difference make?' *English Teaching Forum* 23:4, 2-27.

South African Department of Education and Training. 1986. *Syllabus for Standard Five*. South Africa: Department of Education and Training.

Spindler, G. 1974. 'Beth Anne—A case study of culturally-defined adjustment and teacher perceptions' in G. Spindler (ed.): *Education and Cultural Process*. New York: Holt, Rinehart and Winston.

Sridhar, K. 1982. 'English in a south Indian urban context' in B. Kachru (ed.): *The Other Tongue*. Oxford: Pergamon Press.

Strevens, P. 1987. 'English as an international language.' *English Teaching Forum* 25:4, 56-64.

Sukwiwat, M. 1985. *The Status and Role of English in Thailand*. A Research Report Prepared for the United States Information Agency.

Tanzanian Ministry of National Education. 1982. *English Language Syllabus, Forms V-VI*. Unpublished government document.

Tay, M. 1982. 'The uses, users, and features of English in Singapore' in J. Pride (ed.): *New Englishes*. Rowley, Mass.: Newbury House Publishers.

Todd, L. 1982. 'English in Cameroon: education in a multilingual society' in J. Pride (ed.): *New Englishes*. Rowley, Mass.: Newbury House Publishers.

Trueba, H.I. 1987. 'The ethnography of schooling' in H. Trueba (ed.): *Success or Failure?* New York: Newbury House Publishers.

Trueba, H.T. 1989. *Raising Silent Voices*. New York: Newbury House Publishers.

Trueba, H.T., G.P. Guthrie, and **K.H. Au.** (eds.) 1981. *Culture and the Bilingual Classroom: Studies in Classroom Ethnography*. Rowley, Mass.: Newbury House Publishers.

Unesco. 1953. *The Use of Vernacular Languages in Education: Monographs of Fundamental Education, VII.* Paris: Unesco. Excerpt in J. Fishman: *Readings in the Sociology of Language.* The Hague: Mouton, 1968:688–716.

United States Department of Education. 1987. *Japanese Education Today.* Washington, DC: US Government Printing Office.

Valdes, J.M. (ed.) 1986. *Culture Bound.* Cambridge: Cambridge University Press.

Veno-Kan, L. 1987. *Handbook for Prospective ESL Teachers to Japan.* Unpublished Master's thesis, School for International Training, Brattleboro, Vermont.

Von Schon, C. 1987. 'The question of pronunciation.' *The English Teaching Forum* 25:4, 22–8.

Watson, J.K.P. 1983. 'Cultural pluralism as a national resource: Strategies for language education' in C. Kennedy (ed.): *Language Planning and Language Education.* London: George Allen and Unwin.

Watson-Gegeo, K-A. 1988. 'Ethnography in ESL: Defining the essentials.' *TESOL Quarterly* 22:4, 575–92.

Yates, P. 1986. 'Figure and section: Ethnography and education in the multicultural state' in S. Modgil *et al.* (eds.): *Multicultural Education.* Philadelphia, PA: The Falmer Press.

APPENDIX: SOURCES OF EMPLOYMENT

In general, state-run institutions, particularly elementary and secondary schools, hire local teachers. However, for United States citizens, the United States Peace Corps places English teachers in all levels of public education. The Fulbright Scholar Program offers awards for lecturing, most typically for positions at universities. The United States Information Agency directly administers several teaching programs in many countries. For EC citizens, Voluntary Service Overseas (VSO) places teachers mainly in public secondary schools and teacher-training and tertiary colleges. Addresses for these organizations are listed below.

An employment possibility in the public sector is the British Council, which recruits and administers personnel on a one- or two-year contract basis. There are two departments specializing in recruitment, Central Management of Direct Teaching (CMDT) and the Overseas Educational Appointments Department (OEAD). CMDT administers the Council's network of English language centers which presently number 52 in 31 countries, employing 1,200 staff members. OEAD acts as an agency for the Overseas Development Administration (ODA), recruiting specialists for projects funded under the British Government's aid program. As part of international agreements, OEAD also recruits lecturers for posts in China, republics of the Soviet Union, Mongolia, and Eastern Europe.

Another employment possibility, in the private sector, is American binational centers. In most cases, binational centers are autonomous institutions run by associations of local citizens and American residents with the aim of promoting international understanding. Most binational centers obtain their primary funding from student fees, but they may receive support from the United States government by way of material resources like books and films. Typically these centers hire native speakers of any nationality. Since individual centers differ greatly in their hiring policies, they should be contacted directly to find out about their exact hiring procedures. The United States Information Agency listed below has a complete list.

The British Council, Central Management of Direct Teaching, 10 Spring Gardens, London SW1A 2BN, UK.

The British Council, Overseas Educational Appointments Department, Medlock Street, Manchester M15 4PR, UK.

Fulbright Scholar Lecturing Grants, Council for International Exchange of Scholars, 3007 Tilden Street NW, Suite 5M, Washington, DC 20008–3009, USA.

Peace Corps Recruiting Office, 1900 K Street NW, 9th Floor, Washington, DC 20526, USA.

United States Information Agency, 301 4th Street SW, Washington, DC 20547, USA.

Voluntary Service Overseas, 317 Putney Bridge Road, London SW15 2PG, UK.

INDEX

Entries relate to the introduction, Chapters 1 to 5, and the glossary. References to the glossary are indicated by 'g' after the page number.

curriculum guidelines 80, 85–9, 120–1, 127
Czechoslovakia, English as foreign language 83–4

de-Anglo-Americanizing the curriculum 57–8
determination, language planning 5,6
development, language planning 5,6
Dewan Bahasa dan Pustaka (Language and Literature Agency), Malaysia 14
diglossia 33–5, 137g
  Philippines 37
dimensions of culture 55–8
discipline, policies 116–17, 118, 132–3
discourse differences, New Englishes 92
dissonance, between outside and inside learning 48
distance education 110–11

EAL, *see* English as an auxiliary language
EAP, *see* English for specific purposes
East African Swahili Committee 4
economic context 25–45
economic mobility, association with English 36, 37–8, 40
economic support for language teaching 31–3
education,
  outside and inside the classroom 47–8
  role, cultural views 49
educational goals, effect of sources of funding 113
Educational Resource Information Center (ERIC) 22
education budgets 31
elaboration of language 22
elective subject (English), Japan 101–3
ELWC, *see* English as a language of wider communication
emic perspective 52–4, 58–9
employment,
  factors to be addressed 118–24
  sources 151–2
Engalog 16
English for academic purposes *see* English for specific purposes
English as an auxiliary language (EAL) 137g
English Language Teaching Profiles 22, 43
English as a language of wider communication (ELWC) 11, 28, 137g

English for occupational purposes, *see* English for specific purposes
English for science and technology (EST) 28
  see also English for specific purposes
English as a second language (ESL) 137g
English for specific purposes (ESP) 31, 32, 44, 112, 137g
English teaching institutions 109–35
EOP, *see* English as a second language
ESP, *see* English for specific purposes
EST, *see* English for science and technology
ethnography 52–5, 64–7
etic perspective 53
expanding circle varieties of English 89–90
expectations, classroom 49, 51, 62–8, 71–3, 127
extrinsic and intrinsic sources of motivation 26–7

facilities, institutional 122–4, 128
French,
  in Cameroon 12–13
  in Tunisia 30
Fulbright lecturers 125, 149
funding, teaching institutions 109–13

goals 113, 114–15, 118
  see also objectives
grading policies 116, 117–18
graphization, corpus planning 81
Guatemala, economic support for language teaching 31–2

Hacettepe University, Ankara, Turkey 124–6
High (H) varieties 33–5
  Philippines 37
Honduras, economic support for language teaching 31, 32

implementation, language planning 5–6
India, bilingualism 11
indigenous language(s) 138g
  Uni-modal nations 10
inner circle varieties of English 89–90
  Nigeria 91–2
innovation (semantic), New Englishes 91–2
institutional context 109–35
institutionalized English, *see* nativized English